PROJECT MANAGEMENT UNLEASHED

A Guide for Non-Project Managers to Organize and Excel

By
Gitangshu Adhikary

DEDICATION

To the unsung heroes of the workplace—

This book is dedicated to every employee who juggles endless tasks, meets impossible deadlines, and yet feels their efforts go unnoticed. To those who manage projects without a formal title, who lead without recognition, and who organize chaos into clarity, this is for you.

May *Project Management Unleashed* empower you to harness the tools, techniques, and mindset of project management to not only excel in your work but to transform how you approach challenges, collaborate with teams, and achieve your goals.

To the learners, the doers, and the quiet leaders—you are the cornerstone of success, and your potential is limitless.

ACKNOWLEDGEMENTS

Writing *Project Management Unleashed* has been an incredible journey, one that would not have been possible without the guidance, support, and inspiration of many remarkable individuals.

First, I want to express my deepest gratitude to my readers—the countless non-project managers whose determination to excel in their roles inspired this book. Your drive to bring order to chaos and your willingness to learn and grow are the heartbeat of this work.

To my mentors and colleagues, thank you for sharing your insights and demonstrating the transformative power of effective project management. Your experiences and stories have shaped the practical advice found in these pages.

A special thanks to my family and friends, whose patience and encouragement gave me the confidence to pursue this endeavor. Your unwavering belief in me has always been my greatest strength.

To the pioneers of project management methodologies and the creators of tools like Trello, Asana, and beyond, this book stands on the foundation of your innovation and vision. Thank you for simplifying the complex and empowering individuals to achieve their goals.

Lastly, I want to acknowledge the countless individuals who work behind the scenes to ensure projects succeed, often without recognition. You prove that leadership and impact don't require a title. This book is for you.

PREFACE

When you hear the words *project management*, what comes to mind? A room full of post-it notes? Complex charts and spreadsheets? Or perhaps a specialized skill reserved for trained professionals in corporate settings? For many, project management feels like an intimidating, jargon-filled world—something far removed from their day-to-day responsibilities.

But here's the truth: you're already a project manager. Whether you're planning a team event, launching a marketing campaign, coordinating tasks across departments, or even organizing your personal goals, you're managing projects. And yet, without the right tools and strategies, these projects can feel overwhelming, chaotic, and, at times, unmanageable.

That's where this book comes in. *Project Management Unleashed* was born out of a simple realization: project management is not just for certified professionals. It's a mindset and a skill set that anyone can use to organize their work, collaborate more effectively, and achieve outstanding results. You don't need to master every technical aspect or memorize every methodology to benefit from project management principles. What you need is clarity, structure, and a straightforward guide tailored for those who don't consider themselves project managers—until now.

I've written this book for the marketer juggling multiple campaigns, the small business owner coordinating a dozen moving parts, the HR professional streamlining onboarding, and anyone who wants to bring order to chaos. My goal is to strip away the complexity and offer practical, actionable advice that you can start using immediately.

Over the years, I've worked with teams of all sizes, across

industries, and in diverse roles. What I've discovered is that the principles of project management are universal. It's not about rigid rules or fancy software (though tools do help); it's about adopting a mindset of intentionality and efficiency that empowers you to work smarter, not harder.

This book is divided into digestible sections that walk you through the foundations of project management, the lifecycle of projects, the tools and techniques you'll need, and how to apply these principles to your everyday work. Whether you're leading a team or simply trying to get through your to-do list, this guide will equip you to tackle projects of any size with confidence.

Consider this your invitation to redefine how you approach work. Let's demystify project management, embrace its principles, and unleash your potential to organize and excel—one project at a time.

Welcome to *Project Management Unleashed*. Let's get started.

PART 1: FOUNDATIONS OF PROJECT MANAGEMENT

CHAPTER 1: WHY PROJECT MANAGEMENT MATTERS

Let's start with a simple truth: **project management is everywhere**. From planning a family vacation to coordinating a team presentation at work, you're engaging in project management every day—whether you realize it or not. The good news? When you recognize and embrace this fact, you can transform how you approach your tasks, boost your efficiency, and reduce your stress levels.

Project Management Is for Everyone

You might be thinking, *But I'm not a project manager.* That's okay! You don't need the title to benefit from project management skills. Whether you're an HR professional organizing a recruitment drive, a marketer launching a campaign, or a small business owner juggling client deadlines, project management principles can help you work smarter, not harder.

Think about your typical workday. How often do you find yourself:

- Struggling to prioritize tasks?
- Getting overwhelmed by tight deadlines?
- Feeling like you're always putting out fires instead of working proactively?

Project management offers a solution to these common struggles. It's not just about managing big corporate projects—it's about applying structure and clarity to everything you do.

The Everyday Impact of Project Management

Imagine this: You're hosting a dinner party. You plan the menu, shop for ingredients, cook the dishes, set the table, and time everything so your guests are impressed. That's project management!

Now, picture applying the same structured approach to your work:

- Breaking down large tasks into manageable steps.
- Setting clear timelines and expectations.
- Communicating effectively with everyone involved.

Suddenly, the chaos turns into a well-oiled machine. The result? You feel in control and confident, and the results speak for themselves.

The Big Benefits for Non-Project Managers

So, why does project management matter, especially for non-project managers? Let's dive into the three game-changing benefits:

1. Efficiency: Get More Done in Less Time

With project management techniques, you'll learn how to focus on what truly matters. Instead of jumping between tasks, you'll know exactly what needs to be done, when, and by whom. This clarity saves time and energy, allowing you to accomplish more with less effort.

For instance, creating a simple to-do list with priorities can transform your day. Tools like timelines and checklists keep you on track, ensuring you don't waste hours figuring out your next move.

2. Reduced Stress: Goodbye Chaos, Hello Clarity

Workplace chaos is a stress trigger. Missed deadlines, unclear expectations, and last-minute surprises can leave you feeling frazzled. Project management puts you in the driver's seat.

By organizing tasks, setting realistic deadlines, and anticipating potential roadblocks, you'll feel more prepared and less anxious. It's like turning a stormy sea into a calm, navigable river.

3. Improved Results: Shine in Every Role

At the heart of project management is one goal: **delivering great results.** When you apply its principles, your work doesn't just get done—it gets done well.

Whether you're preparing a report, launching a campaign, or coordinating an event, project management ensures you hit your targets. And when you consistently deliver exceptional results, people notice. It's a career boost waiting to happen.

A Quick Success Story

Meet Anjali, a sales executive at a mid-sized company. Anjali used to feel overwhelmed by her workload—client follow-ups, presentations, and reporting deadlines all piling up. Then, she started applying simple project management principles: she created a daily task list, set realistic deadlines, and used a free project management tool to track her progress.

The result? Anjali began meeting deadlines with ease, her stress levels dropped, and her manager praised her for her efficiency. She even had time to take on a high-visibility special project, further boosting her career.

If Anjali can do it, so can you.

The Power Is in Your Hands

You don't need years of experience or a fancy certification to start reaping the benefits of project management. By adopting a few straightforward techniques, you'll find yourself working more efficiently, staying calm under pressure, and delivering outstanding results.

So, are you ready to take control of your work and unlock your potential? Let's dive deeper into the world of project management—and unleash the productivity powerhouse within you.

CHAPTER 2: PROJECT MANAGEMENT DEMYSTIFIED

Project management often sounds like a buzzword reserved for the boardroom—a mysterious process reserved for people with Gantt charts and clipboards. But here's the reality: **project management isn't rocket science, and it's definitely not exclusive to "project managers."** At its core, it's a practical way to organize work, get things done efficiently, and achieve goals without losing your sanity.

Ready to demystify project management? Let's dive in.

What Is Project Management?

At its simplest, project management is the process of planning, executing, and completing a set of tasks to achieve a specific goal.

Think of it as a roadmap. Instead of wandering aimlessly through your work, you have a clear path that guides you from start to finish. Whether it's launching a new product, planning a wedding, or organizing your workspace, project management turns chaos into clarity.

Here's the key: **Every project has three elements—time, cost, and scope.** These make up the "project management triangle." Your goal is to balance these three:

- **Time:** How long do you have to complete the project?
- **Cost:** What resources (money, people, tools) are available?
- **Scope:** What exactly needs to be done?

Effective project management ensures you stay on course, meeting deadlines, staying within budget, and achieving your objectives without sacrificing quality.

The Key Principles of Project Management

Now that you know what project management is, let's talk about how it works. Successful project management boils down to a handful of guiding principles. These are the secrets that help you stay organized, focused, and effective—every time.

1. Clear Goals: Know Your "Why"

Every project starts with a purpose. Why are you doing this? What does success look like? Without clear goals, even the best-laid plans can go astray.

Take a moment to define your project's objectives. Are you launching a marketing campaign to boost sales by 20%? Are you planning an office event to improve team morale? The clearer your goal, the easier it is to chart a path to success.

2. Planning: The Foundation of Success

Here's a golden rule of project management: **A little planning saves a lot of stress.**

Break down your project into smaller, manageable steps. Assign deadlines, prioritize tasks, and identify potential roadblocks. This doesn't have to be a lengthy process—sometimes a quick brainstorming session or a simple checklist can work wonders.

3. Communication: Keep Everyone in the Loop

Projects rarely happen in isolation. Whether you're working with a team or just coordinating with a few stakeholders, communication is your superpower.

- Set clear expectations for everyone involved.
- Regularly update people on progress.
- Be open to feedback and ready to address concerns.

Think of communication as the glue that holds your project together.

4. Flexibility: Expect the Unexpected

No matter how well you plan, things can—and will—change. A key team member might fall sick, a deadline might shift, or new priorities might emerge. The ability to adapt without losing sight of your goal is what separates great project managers from the rest.

Stay flexible and have a contingency plan. Remember, it's okay to adjust as long as you keep moving forward.

5. Accountability: Own Your Work

Accountability is a cornerstone of effective project management. This doesn't just mean doing your part—it also means ensuring that everyone involved is clear about their responsibilities.

Set milestones and hold yourself (and your team) accountable for hitting them. Celebrate successes along the way, and learn from any missteps.

The Goals of Effective Project Management

Ultimately, project management isn't just about ticking boxes. It's about delivering results while maintaining your sanity and strengthening collaboration. Here are the main goals:

- **Efficiency:** Accomplish more with less effort by focusing on the right tasks at the right time.
- **Clarity:** Eliminate confusion by creating a structured approach to your work.
- **Quality:** Deliver results that meet or exceed expectations.
- **Teamwork:** Build stronger, more productive relationships through clear communication and shared accountability.

Making Project Management Work for You

Here's the beauty of project management: **it's incredibly**

adaptable. Whether you're planning a large-scale corporate initiative or organizing your weekly to-do list, the same principles apply.

Think of it as your personal productivity toolkit. You don't have to use every tool for every project. Start small—identify your goals, create a basic plan, and communicate with those involved. From there, you can refine your approach as you go.

The Myth of the "Perfect Project Manager"

One last thing before we wrap up: You don't have to be perfect to be a good project manager. In fact, some of the best project managers learn through trial and error. The key is to stay curious, keep learning, and never shy away from taking charge of your work.

So, there you have it—project management demystified! With these principles in hand, you're well on your way to taking control of your work and achieving your goals with confidence. Up next, we'll explore the core competencies that can make you a project management pro—even if you're not officially a "project manager." Let's keep going!

CHAPTER 3: CORE COMPETENCIES OF A PROJECT MANAGER

Project management isn't about fancy titles or certifications. At its heart, it's about **skills**—practical, everyday abilities that help you get things done and inspire others to do the same. While there's no one-size-fits-all approach, four core competencies stand out as the pillars of effective project management: **communication, organization, problem-solving, and leadership.**

Here's the best part: **You don't need to be a "project manager" to master these skills.** Whether you're leading a small initiative or contributing to a larger goal, developing these competencies can transform how you work—and how you succeed.

1. Communication: The Lifeline of Any Project

Think of communication as the oxygen your project needs to survive. Without it, even the best plans can fall apart. Clear, concise, and consistent communication ensures that everyone stays informed, engaged, and aligned.

Why It Matters:
- Keeps stakeholders in the loop
- Prevents misunderstandings and confusion
- Builds trust and strengthens collaboration

Key Tips for Non-Project Managers:
- **Practice active listening:** Don't just hear—understand what others are saying. Repeat key points to confirm clarity.

- **Be clear and concise:** Whether in emails or meetings, get to the point. Avoid jargon and focus on what matters.
- **Set expectations early:** Clearly define goals, timelines, and roles from the beginning.
- **Use the right tools:** Platforms like Slack, Zoom, or Microsoft Teams can streamline communication, especially in remote or hybrid settings.

2. Organization: Turning Chaos into Order

A great project manager is like an air traffic controller—keeping everything running smoothly and on time. Organization isn't just about neat to-do lists; it's about creating systems that ensure nothing slips through the cracks.

Why It Matters:
- Reduces overwhelm and keeps projects on track
- Ensures resources (time, money, people) are used effectively
- Helps you prioritize and focus on what's most important

Key Tips for Non-Project Managers:
- **Use visual tools:** Try tools like Trello or Asana to organize tasks and track progress. Even a simple spreadsheet can work wonders.
- **Break projects into chunks:** Divide work into smaller, manageable tasks with clear deadlines.
- **Create a daily plan:** Start each day with a clear list of priorities.
- **Review regularly:** Check your progress often and adjust as needed.

3. Problem-Solving: Your Secret Weapon

No project goes exactly as planned. Challenges will arise—that's a guarantee. What sets successful project managers apart is their ability to tackle problems head-on, staying calm under pressure and finding creative solutions.

Why It Matters:
- Keeps projects moving forward despite obstacles

- Builds resilience and adaptability
- Encourages innovation and new ideas

Key Tips for Non-Project Managers:
- **Identify the root cause:** Don't just treat symptoms—dig deeper to understand what's really causing the issue.
- **Brainstorm solutions:** Involve your team or colleagues in generating ideas. Two (or more) heads are always better than one.
- **Stay calm and focused:** Panic never solves anything. Take a deep breath, assess the situation, and act methodically.
- **Learn from setbacks:** Every challenge is an opportunity to grow. Reflect on what went wrong and how to avoid it in the future.

4. Leadership: Inspiring Others to Succeed

Leadership isn't about having all the answers or being the loudest voice in the room. It's about empowering others, creating a shared vision, and motivating your team to reach the finish line together.

Why It Matters:
- Fosters collaboration and teamwork
- Encourages accountability and ownership
- Builds a positive, productive work environment

Key Tips for Non-Project Managers:
- **Lead by example:** Show, don't tell. Demonstrate the behaviors you want others to emulate—whether it's punctuality, professionalism, or problem-solving.
- **Be empathetic:** Understand the needs and concerns of your colleagues. A little empathy goes a long way.
- **Celebrate wins:** Acknowledge and appreciate the efforts of your team. Recognition is a powerful motivator.
- **Empower others:** Delegate tasks, trust your team, and encourage them to take ownership of their work.

How to Develop These Skills as a Non-Project Manager

The beauty of these competencies is that they're not exclusive to project managers. They're life skills—ones you can develop and refine in everyday situations.

Start Small:
- Practice communicating more effectively in your emails or team meetings.
- Organize your daily tasks using a planner or digital tool.
- Approach small challenges with a problem-solving mindset.
- Take initiative in group projects, even if you're not in charge.

Learn Continuously:
- Read books, attend workshops, or take online courses focused on these skills.
- Seek feedback from colleagues and mentors to identify areas for improvement.

Apply What You Learn:

The best way to master these skills is through practice. Volunteer to lead a small project, organize a team event, or take charge of a new task. Every experience is an opportunity to grow.

The Power of Core Competencies

When you develop these four core competencies—communication, organization, problem-solving, and leadership—you're not just improving your ability to manage projects. You're enhancing your ability to manage yourself, your relationships, and your career.

These skills aren't just for the workplace—they're for life. Whether you're planning a family vacation, organizing a fundraiser, or navigating a personal goal, the principles of project management will serve you well.

So, take a moment to reflect: Which of these skills do you already excel at? Which ones could use some attention? With a little effort and practice, you can master them all—and unlock your full potential as a project management pro, no matter your role.

Let's keep building on this momentum! Next, we'll explore the different frameworks and methodologies that can help you put these skills into action. Ready to dive into the world of Waterfall and Agile? Let's go!

CHAPTER 4: THE ROLE OF NON-PROJECT MANAGERS IN PROJECT SUCCESS

You may not wear the "project manager" hat, but make no mistake: **your role in a project's success is invaluable.** Whether you're a designer, analyst, marketer, or admin, your contribution shapes the outcome just as much as the person overseeing the plan. In fact, projects thrive when every team member understands their impact and takes ownership of their part.

Let's unpack the ways **non-project managers can be the unsung heroes** of any project and explore real-world stories of individuals like you stepping up and making a difference.

Understanding Your Impact

Picture this: A project is like a symphony. The project manager is the conductor, setting the tempo and ensuring every instrument plays in harmony. But the music wouldn't exist without the violinists, drummers, and flutists—each adding their unique sound. As a non-project manager, you're one of those key players.

Why Your Role Matters:

1. **You're the subject matter expert.**
   Your knowledge and expertise often drive the project's content or deliverables. Whether it's creating a product

design or drafting a report, your contributions are the foundation.

2. **You're the problem-solver.**
When challenges arise, you're often the first to spot them. Your insights help the team course-correct before issues snowball.

3. **You're the bridge-builder.**
Projects often involve cross-functional collaboration. Your ability to communicate and connect with others —whether it's teammates, vendors, or stakeholders— keeps the project flowing smoothly.

4. **You're the implementer.**
While the project manager focuses on the bigger picture, you're in the trenches, ensuring tasks are executed with precision and care.

Your Role in Action: Real-World Examples

Let's take a look at how non-project managers have stepped up, embraced project management techniques, and driven projects to success.

Case Study 1: A Marketing Specialist Organizes a Campaign

Meet Ananya, a marketing specialist tasked with running her company's first-ever virtual product launch. She wasn't a project manager, but she knew the stakes were high.

- **What She Did:**
    - Broke down the campaign into smaller tasks: planning the launch video, setting up the webinar, creating social media posts.
    - Used a free tool like Trello to assign deadlines and keep track of progress.
    - Communicated regularly with her team, ensuring everyone stayed on the same page.
- **The Result:**
The campaign launched without a hitch, earning rave

reviews from clients and increasing product sales by 40%.

- **Takeaway:**
  By applying basic project management principles, Ananya turned a daunting task into a manageable—and successful—campaign.

Case Study 2: An IT Analyst Streamlines a System Upgrade

Raj, an IT analyst, was asked to oversee a major system upgrade alongside his usual responsibilities. While he didn't consider himself a project manager, he decided to approach the task like one.

- **What He Did:**
  - Created a timeline with clear milestones, such as testing, deployment, and user training.
  - Held weekly check-ins with the team to address roadblocks and update progress.
  - Documented lessons learned along the way to improve future upgrades.
- **The Result:**
  The upgrade was completed ahead of schedule, with minimal downtime. Raj's proactive approach earned praise from both his manager and colleagues.
- **Takeaway:**
  Raj's ability to organize, communicate, and track progress proved that you don't need a formal title to lead a project effectively.

How You Can Thrive as a Non-Project Manager

If you're ready to take ownership of your role and make an even bigger impact, here are some actionable tips to get started:

1. Embrace Ownership

Don't wait for someone to assign you tasks. Take initiative, ask questions, and seek clarity on how your work fits into the bigger picture.

2. Learn to Prioritize

Not all tasks are created equal. Focus on high-impact activities that move the project forward and align with its goals.

3. Communicate Often

Keep your project manager and teammates informed of your progress, challenges, and ideas. Proactive communication builds trust and prevents misunderstandings.

4. Use Tools and Techniques

Adopt simple project management tools like to-do lists, timelines, or apps (e.g., Asana, Monday.com). These can help you stay organized and efficient.

5. Stay Flexible

Projects rarely go as planned. Be open to change, adapt quickly, and approach new challenges with a problem-solving mindset.

The Ripple Effect of Your Contributions

When you bring your A-game to a project, the impact goes beyond just meeting deadlines or hitting targets. You:

- **Build trust:** Your proactive approach earns the respect of your peers and managers.
- **Foster collaboration:** Your contributions create a positive, productive team dynamic.
- **Grow professionally:** By stepping up, you develop valuable skills that enhance your career trajectory.

Remember, successful projects aren't about one person leading the charge—they're about teams working together, with each member playing their part to perfection. And that includes you.

The Big Picture: Why You Matter

Even if you're not "in charge," your role in a project is just as crucial as the project manager's. You bring expertise, energy, and execution power to the table—qualities that can make or break a project's success.

So, the next time you're part of a project, don't underestimate your value. Embrace your role, apply the tips and techniques you're learning, and watch as your contributions elevate not just the project—but also your professional growth.

Ready to learn how to tackle projects using proven methodologies like Waterfall and Agile? The next chapter will break them down and show you how to choose the right approach for your needs.

PART 2: PROJECT MANAGEMENT FRAMEWORKS AND METHODOLOGIES

CHAPTER 5: TWO STYLES: WATERFALL VS. AGILE

When it comes to project management, choosing the right methodology can feel like picking between two powerful tools in a toolbox. Both Waterfall and Agile have their strengths, but each serves a different purpose. By understanding these methodologies, you can select the one that fits your project like a glove—or even blend the two for maximum impact.

Let's dive into the world of Waterfall and Agile, breaking down what they are, how they work, and when you should use each one.

The Waterfall Methodology: A Step-by-Step Journey

Think of Waterfall as a well-organized assembly line. Each phase of the project flows into the next like water cascading down a series of steps—hence the name.

How It Works:

Waterfall follows a linear, sequential process.

1. **Initiation:** Define the project's goals and requirements upfront.
2. **Planning:** Develop a detailed plan, including timelines, budgets, and deliverables.
3. **Execution:** Carry out the work according to the plan.
4. **Monitoring:** Track progress and ensure everything stays on schedule.
5. **Closing:** Wrap up the project, deliver the results, and review

lessons learned.

The Pros:
- **Clarity:** Clear phases and milestones mean everyone knows what's expected and when.
- **Thorough planning:** Everything is mapped out in detail before work begins.
- **Predictability:** Ideal for projects with fixed requirements, like construction or manufacturing.

The Cons:
- **Rigidity:** Once the plan is set, changes can be hard (and expensive) to implement.
- **Delayed feedback:** Problems may only surface late in the process.
- **Not ideal for evolving projects:** If requirements change, Waterfall can feel like steering a ship with no rudder.

When to Use Waterfall:

Waterfall shines in projects where requirements are clear, stable, and unlikely to change. Examples include:
- Building a house
- Designing hardware
- Publishing a book with a set deadline

The Agile Methodology: A Flexible Adventure

If Waterfall is a carefully plotted roadmap, Agile is like navigating with a compass—flexible, adaptable, and iterative. Agile thrives on collaboration and feedback, making it ideal for dynamic projects.

How It Works:

Agile is based on incremental progress. Work is divided into small, manageable chunks called **sprints** (usually lasting 1–4 weeks).

1. **Plan:** Start with high-level goals and prioritize tasks.
2. **Execute:** Complete a small portion of the project in each sprint.
3. **Review:** Gather feedback from stakeholders and adjust as

needed.
4. **Repeat:** Iterate until the final product is complete.

The Pros:
- **Flexibility:** Easily adapt to changing requirements.
- **Continuous feedback:** Regular reviews keep everyone aligned.
- **Faster delivery:** Small increments mean you can deliver value sooner.

The Cons:
- **Less predictability:** Fluid plans can be hard to pin down.
- **Requires collaboration:** Agile thrives on communication and teamwork—if these falter, so does the project.
- **Learning curve:** It may take time for teams to fully embrace Agile practices.

When to Use Agile:

Agile excels in projects with evolving requirements or where innovation is key. Examples include:
- Software development
- Marketing campaigns
- Research and development

Waterfall vs. Agile: Which Should You Choose?

The choice between Waterfall and Agile depends on your project's nature, goals, and constraints. Here's a quick comparison to help you decide:

Feature	Waterfall	Agile
Structure	Linear, sequential	Iterative, flexible
Best For	Fixed requirements	Evolving requirements
Planning	Detailed, upfront	High-level, ongoing
Feedback	At the end	Continuous
Adaptability	Limited	High

Real-Life Examples: Choosing the Right Approach

Scenario 1: Building a Website for a Client
- **Waterfall Fit:** If the client provides exact specifications upfront and doesn't expect changes.
- **Agile Fit:** If the client wants to see early drafts, provide feedback, and tweak the design as you go.

Scenario 2: Launching a New Product
- **Waterfall Fit:** If the product is based on a fixed formula (e.g., manufacturing a car).
- **Agile Fit:** If the product involves testing and adapting to user feedback (e.g., a mobile app).

Scenario 3: Planning an Office Move
- **Waterfall Fit:** With a fixed moving date and specific logistical requirements.
- **Agile Fit:** If the move involves multiple phases and ongoing feedback (e.g., updating spaces after feedback).

Can You Combine Both?

Absolutely! Many projects benefit from a **hybrid approach** that takes the best of both worlds:
- Use Waterfall for the high-level plan (e.g., setting deadlines, budgets).
- Use Agile for specific phases (e.g., testing and tweaking a product).

This hybrid model is especially useful for complex projects with a mix of stable and evolving elements.

Final Thoughts: Embrace the Method That Fits You Best

Waterfall and Agile aren't competitors—they're tools, and the right one depends on the job at hand. By understanding these methodologies, you'll be better equipped to approach any project with confidence and clarity.

So, the next time you're faced with a project, ask yourself:
- Are the requirements clear and unchanging? **Waterfall might be your go-to.**

- Are flexibility and iteration key? **Agile could be your best bet.**

Ready to take a deeper dive into applying these methods in real-world projects? In the next chapter, we'll explore the phases of a project lifecycle, from kick-off to closing, with practical tips for staying organized and on track. Let's keep the momentum going!

CHAPTER 6: THE WATERFALL APPROACH: A STEP-BY-STEP PROCESS

The Waterfall approach is the grandmaster of structure in project management—a methodology that thrives on clarity and precision. If you love a well-organized plan with clear steps and no surprises, Waterfall might just be your project management soulmate.

In this chapter, we'll break down the Waterfall methodology into its five core phases and explore when it's the best tool for the job. Whether you're managing a big work project or organizing a family event, Waterfall principles can help you get things done smoothly and effectively.

The Five Phases of Waterfall

Waterfall is like following a recipe: each step builds on the last, and you don't move forward until the current phase is complete. Let's dive into the phases:

1. Initiation: Laying the Foundation

Every successful project begins with a strong foundation. In the initiation phase, your goal is to answer three crucial questions:

- **What is the project?** Define the purpose and scope clearly.

- **Why is it important?** Understand its value to stakeholders or the organization.
- **What are the constraints?** Identify time, budget, and resource limits.

Key Actions:
- Draft a project charter that outlines goals, deliverables, and key stakeholders.
- Conduct a feasibility study to ensure the project is worth pursuing.
- Secure approvals and resources to move forward.

Real-World Example:

Imagine you're tasked with setting up a new office space. The initiation phase involves deciding on the location, budget, and timeline—and getting buy-in from decision-makers.

2. Planning: Creating the Blueprint

Now it's time to get detailed. The planning phase is where you outline every step of the project, ensuring nothing is left to chance.

Key Actions:
- Develop a detailed project plan, including:
    - A timeline with milestones and deadlines.
    - Task breakdowns and dependencies (what needs to happen before the next step).
    - Resource allocation (who will do what and when).
- Identify potential risks and create contingency plans.

Pro Tip:

Use tools like Gantt charts or project management software to visualize your plan and keep track of progress.

Real-World Example:

For the office move, this phase involves deciding which furniture to buy, scheduling movers, and planning IT setup—all while ensuring the team can transition smoothly.

3. Execution: Bringing the Plan to Life

With your plan in place, it's time to get to work. The execution phase is all about turning plans into action.

Key Actions:
- Assign tasks to team members and ensure everyone knows their roles.
- Communicate regularly to keep everyone aligned.
- Manage resources efficiently to avoid bottlenecks.

Pro Tip:

While Waterfall emphasizes following the plan, stay open to minor adjustments. Address issues as they arise to keep the project on track.

Real-World Example:

This is when movers are shifting furniture, contractors are setting up cubicles, and IT is installing systems. You're overseeing it all to ensure smooth progress.

4. Monitoring: Staying on Track

Even with the best plan, projects rarely run themselves. Monitoring ensures the project stays on schedule, within budget, and aligned with goals.

Key Actions:
- Track progress against the project plan using dashboards or status reports.
- Identify deviations (delays, overspending) and take corrective action.
- Keep stakeholders informed through regular updates.

Pro Tip:

Schedule weekly check-ins to review progress, address issues, and make adjustments if necessary.

Real-World Example:

For the office move, monitoring might involve checking that furniture arrives on time, ensuring movers stick to the schedule, and confirming that IT systems are functional before staff arrives.

5. Closing: Wrapping It Up

Once the work is done, the closing phase ensures you leave no loose ends. Celebrate the project's completion while taking the time to reflect on what worked and what didn't.

Key Actions:
- Deliver the final product or service to stakeholders.
- Conduct a project review to capture lessons learned.
- Archive documentation for future reference.

Pro Tip:

End on a high note by celebrating the team's success, no matter how small the project. Acknowledge individual contributions to boost morale.

Real-World Example:

For the office move, closing involves conducting a final walkthrough, ensuring everything is operational, and gathering feedback from employees about their new workspace.

When Waterfall Works Best

Waterfall thrives in situations where structure and predictability are key. Here are some scenarios where it's the ideal choice:

1. **Fixed Requirements:** Projects where goals and deliverables are clear from the start.
    - Example: Designing a product based on established specifications.
2. **Tight Timelines:** When missing a deadline isn't an option.
    - Example: Publishing a book before the holiday season.
3. **Regulatory Compliance:** Industries like healthcare or construction where processes must follow strict standards.
    - Example: Building a hospital that meets safety codes.

The Waterfall Advantage

Waterfall is a classic for a reason. Its structured approach provides:

- **Clarity:** Everyone knows what to do and when.
- **Predictability:** Timelines and budgets are easier to manage.
- **Accountability:** Defined roles and responsibilities keep the team focused.

Final Thoughts: Embrace the Structure

Waterfall isn't just a methodology—it's a mindset. When applied to the right projects, it can create a seamless workflow that takes you from idea to completion with confidence.

In the next chapter, we'll explore a very different (and equally exciting) approach: Agile. If Waterfall is about structure, Agile is about flexibility. Ready to pivot, iterate, and adapt? Let's dive in!

CHAPTER 7: THE AGILE APPROACH: FLEXIBILITY AND ITERATION

Imagine a world where change isn't a roadblock but an opportunity—a world where adaptability is the star of the show. Welcome to Agile, a project management methodology designed for dynamic environments where priorities can shift, feedback is constant, and collaboration drives results.

In this chapter, we'll demystify Agile's core concepts and explore its real-world applications. If you've ever felt stuck in rigid plans that don't align with evolving needs, Agile might just become your favorite new approach.

What is Agile?

Agile is all about being nimble, fast, and responsive. It's a project management framework rooted in collaboration and iteration. Unlike Waterfall's linear process, Agile embraces flexibility, allowing teams to adjust their course as they go.

At its heart, Agile revolves around four key values (based on the **Agile Manifesto**):

1. **Individuals and interactions** over processes and tools.
2. **Working solutions** over comprehensive documentation.
3. **Customer collaboration** over contract negotiation.

4. **Responding to change** over following a plan.

The Agile Toolbox: Key Concepts

1. Sprints: Bite-Sized Progress

In Agile, work is divided into short, focused intervals called **sprints**, typically lasting 1-4 weeks. Each sprint delivers a specific, tangible outcome—a feature, a prototype, or a solution.

How Sprints Work:

- **Plan:** At the start of each sprint, the team decides what they'll accomplish.
- **Execute:** Work happens within the sprint, with team members collaborating daily.
- **Deliver:** At the end, the team presents their progress for feedback.

Pro Tip:

Keep sprints short and sweet. The goal is progress, not perfection.

2. Stand-Ups: Daily Alignment

Stand-up meetings (or daily scrums) are brief, high-energy check-ins where the team answers three key questions:

1. **What did I accomplish yesterday?**
2. **What will I focus on today?**
3. **What obstacles are in my way?**

Why Stand-Ups Matter:

- They keep everyone aligned and accountable.
- They uncover blockers early, so the team can address them promptly.

Pro Tip:

Limit stand-ups to 15 minutes. Stay standing—literally! It keeps the meeting focused.

3. Retrospectives: Learning and Improving

At the end of each sprint, teams hold a **retrospective** to reflect on what went well, what didn't, and how they can improve. It's an opportunity to celebrate successes, address challenges, and refine processes.

Why Retrospectives Matter:
- They foster a culture of continuous improvement.
- They create a safe space for feedback and growth.

Pro Tip:

Use tools like a "Start, Stop, Continue" board to structure discussions:
- **Start:** New practices to try.
- **Stop:** What isn't working.
- **Continue:** What's going well.

When to Use Agile

Agile thrives in fast-paced, ever-changing environments. Here are some scenarios where Agile shines:

1. **Evolving Requirements:**
   - Agile is perfect when the end goal isn't crystal clear from the start or when priorities may shift.
   - **Example:** Developing a new app where user feedback drives features.

2. **Complex Projects with High Uncertainty:**
   - For projects with multiple moving parts, Agile allows teams to focus on smaller, manageable pieces.
   - **Example:** Launching a marketing campaign that requires input from different teams and quick pivots.

3. **Collaborative, Cross-Functional Teams:**
   - Agile fosters collaboration between diverse skill sets.
   - **Example:** Creating a product that involves designers, developers, and marketers working together.

The Agile Advantage

Here's why Agile is a game-changer for many teams:
- **Flexibility:** Plans adapt as needs change, ensuring relevance and effectiveness.
- **Faster Results:** Regular deliveries mean stakeholders see progress sooner.
- **Improved Collaboration:** Team members communicate and collaborate more effectively.
- **Customer-Centric:** Agile prioritizes end-user needs and feedback.

Agile in Action: A Real-World Example

Let's say you're planning a community fundraiser. Instead of locking in every detail upfront, you use Agile:
- **Sprint 1:** Secure the venue and create a draft program.
- **Sprint 2:** Confirm speakers and set up a registration system.
- **Sprint 3:** Promote the event and finalize logistics.
  With each sprint, you adjust based on feedback—perhaps switching venues or refining the agenda. By the time the event rolls around, it's polished, thanks to Agile's iterative approach.

Final Thoughts: Embrace the Agile Mindset

Agile isn't just a methodology; it's a mindset of adaptability, collaboration, and progress. Whether you're leading a team or managing your own workload, Agile offers tools to stay flexible and productive.

Next, we'll dive into the practicalities of starting a project—the kickoff phase where ideas take shape and plans begin.

PART 3: THE PROJECT LIFECYCLE

CHAPTER 8: GETTING STARTED: PROJECT KICK-OFF

Every great project starts with a strong foundation. A successful project kickoff isn't just about diving into tasks—it's about building clarity, alignment, and excitement. Whether you're leading a team or working solo, this phase is your chance to set the stage for success.

In this chapter, we'll explore how to establish clear objectives, define what success looks like, and engage stakeholders from the get-go. Think of this as the launchpad for your project's journey—get it right, and the rest will flow smoothly.

Why the Kick-off Matters

The kickoff is the moment where ideas transform into action. Without a strong kickoff, you risk starting on shaky ground. Misaligned expectations, unclear goals, and disengaged stakeholders can derail even the best intentions.

A great kickoff, on the other hand, ensures that:
- Everyone knows the project's purpose and priorities.
- Stakeholders feel invested in the outcome.
- The team has a roadmap for navigating the journey ahead.

So let's dive into how to make your kickoff count.

Step 1: Setting Clear Objectives

A project without clear objectives is like a road trip without a map. Where are you headed? What milestones will you pass along the way? Defining your objectives is crucial for maintaining focus and measuring progress.

How to Define Clear Objectives
1. **Start with the Big Picture:**
    - Ask yourself, *Why are we doing this project?*
    - Example: For a marketing campaign, the big-picture goal might be to increase brand awareness.
2. **Get Specific:**
    - Break down the big goal into specific, measurable objectives.
    - Example: Instead of "Increase brand awareness," try "Grow social media followers by 20% in three months."
3. **Use the SMART Framework:**
    - **Specific:** Clearly define what you want to achieve.
    - **Measurable:** Include metrics to track progress.
    - **Achievable:** Set realistic goals.
    - **Relevant:** Align with broader organizational priorities.
    - **Time-bound:** Set deadlines.

Pro Tip:

Write down your objectives and share them with everyone involved. When everyone understands the "why," the "how" becomes much easier.

Step 2: Defining Success

Success looks different for every project. What does "done" mean for your project? And what does *successful* look like beyond just completion?

Questions to Define Success:
- What outcomes are we aiming for?
- How will we measure these outcomes?

- Who defines success—the team, the client, the end-user?

Example:

For a website redesign project:
- Completion: The site is live and functional.
- Success: User engagement increases by 30% within the first three months.

Pro Tip:

Don't just focus on hard metrics like numbers. Consider qualitative outcomes too, like improved user experience or team collaboration.

Step 3: Engaging Stakeholders

Stakeholders are anyone who has an interest in your project—team members, clients, managers, or even end-users. Getting them on board early is critical. The more invested they are, the smoother your project will run.

Who Are Your Stakeholders?

- **Primary Stakeholders:** People directly involved in or impacted by the project (e.g., team members, clients).
- **Secondary Stakeholders:** Those indirectly affected (e.g., other departments, senior leadership).

How to Engage Stakeholders

1. **Communicate Early and Often:**
   - Share the project's objectives and goals upfront.
   - Keep communication open throughout the project.
2. **Understand Their Needs:**
   - Ask stakeholders what they expect from the project.
   - Address any concerns or priorities they have.
3. **Involve Them in Planning:**
   - Invite stakeholders to participate in brainstorming sessions or planning meetings.
   - When people contribute to the plan, they feel more

invested in its success.
4. **Set Clear Expectations:**
    - Define everyone's role and responsibilities.
    - Clarify how and when stakeholders will receive updates.

Kick-off in Action: A Real-World Example

Imagine you're planning an office-wide charity event. Here's how the kickoff might look:

1. **Objective:** Raise $10,000 for a local cause by hosting a fundraiser.
2. **Success:** Achieving the monetary goal and receiving positive feedback from attendees.
3. **Stakeholders:**
    - Primary: Event planning committee, volunteers.
    - Secondary: Office leadership, the charity organization.
4. **Engagement:**
    - Schedule a kickoff meeting to align on objectives.
    - Assign roles: someone to handle logistics, another for promotion, etc.
    - Share a progress tracker to keep everyone updated.

Common Kick-off Mistakes to Avoid

1. **Skipping the Objectives:**
    - Without clear goals, the project can quickly lose direction.
2. **Ignoring Stakeholders:**
    - Stakeholders who feel left out can become roadblocks later.
3. **Overloading the Kickoff Meeting:**
    - Keep it concise—focus on the essentials and save details for later discussions.

Final Thoughts: Set the Tone for Success

A great kickoff sets the tone for the entire project. By clarifying objectives, defining success, and engaging stakeholders, you're building a foundation that can weather challenges and deliver results.

Now that you've got your project off the ground, it's time to move into the nitty-gritty: planning phases, timelines, and tasks. In the next chapter, we'll explore how to outline your project like a pro—stay tuned!

CHAPTER 9: PLANNING LIKE A PRO: OUTLINING PHASES AND TASKS

Planning might not sound glamorous, but it's the heartbeat of any successful project. Think of it as laying the train tracks before the locomotive starts moving. Without a solid plan, even the best ideas can derail. In this chapter, we'll break down how to structure your project into manageable phases and tasks, set priorities, and identify dependencies.

Grab your metaphorical hard hat—let's get building!

Why Break Down the Work?

Big projects can feel overwhelming, like staring up at a towering mountain. Breaking work into smaller, manageable phases is like creating a clear trail with well-marked milestones. It keeps you focused, reduces stress, and helps you celebrate progress along the way.

A well-planned project:

- Keeps the team aligned and motivated.
- Helps you spot potential roadblocks early.
- Ensures nothing important falls through the cracks.

Let's dive into how to break it all down.

Step 1: Divide the Project into Phases

A phase is a chunk of work that represents a distinct stage of your project. Most projects follow a natural progression, even if they vary in complexity.

The Common Phases:
1. **Initiation:** Defining objectives, success criteria, and stakeholders.
2. **Planning:** Creating the roadmap.
3. **Execution:** Doing the actual work.
4. **Monitoring:** Tracking progress and making adjustments.
5. **Closing:** Wrapping up and reviewing.

Each phase builds on the previous one. Skipping a phase (or rushing through it) can lead to missteps later.

Example:

Project: Launching a New Product
- **Initiation:** Research market needs, define goals.
- **Planning:** Develop the product roadmap, assign tasks.
- **Execution:** Build the product and test prototypes.
- **Monitoring:** Track progress and adjust based on feedback.
- **Closing:** Launch the product and review outcomes.

Breaking your project into phases gives you a bird's-eye view of the journey ahead.

Step 2: Break Phases into Tasks

Once you have your phases, it's time to get granular. Tasks are the individual action items that make up each phase. Think of tasks as the building blocks of your project.

Tips for Effective Task Breakdown:
1. **Be Specific:**
    - Tasks should describe a single, actionable step.
    - Example: Instead of "Write report," try "Draft first three sections of the report."

2. **Keep Tasks Manageable:**
   - A task should take hours or days, not weeks.
   - If it feels too big, break it down further.
3. **Use Action Words:**
   - Start tasks with verbs like "write," "design," "review," or "update."

Example:
Phase: Product Testing
- Test initial prototype.
- Collect user feedback.
- Revise based on feedback.
- Finalize testing.

Clear, manageable tasks make it easy for you (and your team) to stay on track.

Step 3: Set Priorities

Not all tasks are created equal. Some are mission-critical, while others are nice-to-haves. Prioritizing tasks ensures you're always focusing on what matters most.

The Eisenhower Matrix:
A simple tool to prioritize tasks based on urgency and importance.
1. **Urgent & Important:** Do these first.
2. **Important, Not Urgent:** Schedule these.
3. **Urgent, Not Important:** Delegate these.
4. **Not Urgent & Not Important:** Consider skipping these.

Example:
Scenario: Preparing for a Conference
- Urgent & Important: Confirm venue.
- Important, Not Urgent: Design promotional materials.
- Urgent, Not Important: Respond to minor attendee inquiries.
- Not Urgent & Not Important: Choose table decorations.

This framework helps you focus your energy where it matters

most.

Step 4: Identify Dependencies

Tasks don't exist in isolation—many depend on each other. Understanding these relationships is critical for smooth progress.

Types of Dependencies:

1. **Finish-to-Start (FS):** Task B can't start until Task A is done.
    - Example: You can't paint the walls until the primer is dry.
2. **Start-to-Start (SS):** Task B can start when Task A begins.
    - Example: Testing can begin while coding is still ongoing.
3. **Finish-to-Finish (FF):** Task B must finish at the same time as Task A.
    - Example: Editing and proofreading often overlap.

How to Manage Dependencies:

- Use project management tools (e.g., Trello, Asana) to visualize dependencies.
- Clearly communicate task relationships to your team.
- Plan buffer time for tasks with tight dependencies.

Real-World Example:

Scenario: Planning a Team Retreat

- **Phase:** Booking logistics.
    - Task: Research venues.
    - Task: Get budget approval (dependent on research).
    - Task: Book the venue (dependent on approval).

Mapping out dependencies avoids bottlenecks and ensures a smoother process.

Common Planning Pitfalls to Avoid:

1. **Overloading Phases:** Trying to do too much in one phase can

cause burnout.
2. **Skipping Prioritization:** Without priorities, you risk wasting time on low-impact tasks.
3. **Ignoring Dependencies:** Overlooking relationships between tasks can lead to delays.

Final Thoughts: The Art of Planning

Planning isn't about creating a rigid blueprint—it's about building a flexible framework that guides your project toward success. By breaking work into phases, setting priorities, and mapping dependencies, you're not just organizing tasks; you're creating a clear, actionable roadmap.

With your planning skills honed, you're ready for the next step: keeping timelines and deadlines on track. Let's tackle that in the upcoming chapter—stay tuned!

CHAPTER 10: TIMELINES AND DEADLINES: KEEPING THE PROJECT ON TRACK

Deadlines. Love them or hate them, they're what keep projects moving forward. A well-thought-out timeline is like your project's GPS—it tells you where you're going, how long it'll take, and what to expect along the way. But let's be real: even the best-laid plans can hit unexpected detours. In this chapter, we'll master the art of creating realistic schedules and learn how to adapt when life throws a wrench into your plans.

Grab your calendar, and let's make scheduling work for you!

The Power of a Realistic Schedule

A good timeline doesn't just get you to the finish line—it ensures you arrive with your sanity intact. Unrealistic schedules lead to burnout, missed deadlines, and unnecessary stress. On the flip side, a thoughtful timeline:

- Provides clarity for you and your team.
- Keeps everyone accountable.
- Reduces last-minute chaos.

Think of your schedule as the backbone of your project. Strong, flexible, and built to last.

Step 1: Start with the End in Mind

Every great project timeline begins with the destination. Ask yourself:
- What is the ultimate goal?
- When is the project due?
- Are there external deadlines (e.g., client deliverables or event dates)?

By anchoring your timeline to a clear end date, you can work backward to set realistic milestones.

Example:

Project: Launching a Marketing Campaign
- **End Goal:** Campaign goes live on April 30.
- **Work Backward:**
    - April 15: Finalize all materials.
    - April 1: Conduct testing and reviews.
    - March 15: Draft content and designs.

Step 2: Break It Down

Timelines are more manageable when you divide them into smaller chunks. Use the project phases you outlined earlier (Initiation, Planning, Execution, Monitoring, and Closing) and assign timeframes to each phase.

Tips for Breaking Down Timelines:
1. **Be Specific:** Assign dates to each phase or task. Avoid vague timeframes like "next month."
2. **Include Buffers:** Add extra time for tasks that might take longer than expected.
3. **Identify Milestones:** These are key checkpoints that show you're on track.

Example:

Phase: Content Creation for Campaign

- March 1-5: Brainstorm ideas.
- March 6-10: Write drafts.
- March 11-14: Review and revise.

Breaking tasks into time blocks keeps things clear and achievable.

Step 3: Tools for Scheduling

Gone are the days of juggling sticky notes or messy spreadsheets. Today, there's a treasure trove of tools to make scheduling a breeze.

Popular Tools:
- **Trello:** Visual boards for tracking tasks and deadlines.
- **Asana:** Ideal for collaborative timelines.
- **Google Calendar:** Simple but effective for tracking deadlines.
- **Gantt Charts:** Visualize tasks, timelines, and dependencies.

Pick the tool that fits your style and get started.

Handling the Unexpected: Adjusting Your Schedule

No matter how perfect your plan, life happens. Deadlines shift, priorities change, and unforeseen obstacles pop up. The key is learning to adjust without losing momentum.

Common Challenges and Solutions:

1. **Missed Deadlines:**
   - **Why it Happens:** Overestimating capacity or unexpected delays.
   - **Solution:** Reassess the timeline. Adjust future tasks to compensate, and communicate changes to stakeholders promptly.

2. **Scope Creep:**
   - **Why it Happens:** New tasks or goals are added mid-project.
   - **Solution:** Reevaluate priorities. Either extend the timeline or adjust the scope to stay on track.

3. **Resource Constraints:**

- **Why it Happens:** Team members fall sick, tools fail, or budgets shrink.
- **Solution:** Identify alternative resources or reassign tasks to keep moving forward.

The Art of Flexibility

Adapting your schedule doesn't mean you've failed—it means you're resourceful. Here's how to stay flexible while keeping the project on track:

1. **Revisit Priorities:** Focus on high-impact tasks and push lower-priority items.
2. **Communicate Early:** Keep stakeholders informed of changes to avoid surprises.
3. **Celebrate Progress:** Even small wins can boost morale when timelines shift.

Example:

Scenario: A critical team member is unavailable.

- Reassign their tasks temporarily.
- Shift deadlines for non-critical items.
- Use the buffer time you built into your schedule.

Case Study: Turning a Crisis into Opportunity

Meet Priya, a marketing manager tasked with organizing a product launch. Midway through the project, supply chain delays threatened to derail the timeline. Instead of panicking, Priya:

1. Reassessed the timeline and extended the launch by one week.
2. Communicated the new schedule to her team and stakeholders.
3. Used the extra time to refine the promotional materials.

The result? The product launched smoothly, and the delay actually improved the campaign's quality.

Final Thoughts: Timelines That Work for You

Creating a realistic timeline is more than just setting deadlines—it's about building a roadmap that keeps you and your team focused, flexible, and motivated.

Remember:
- Start with the end in mind.
- Break the work into manageable chunks.
- Use tools to stay organized.
- Be ready to adapt when needed.

With a strong timeline in place, you're ready to move confidently into the execution phase of your project. Deadlines won't feel like the enemy—they'll be your guiding star. Let's keep the momentum going!

CHAPTER 11: ASSIGNING ROLES AND RESPONSIBILITIES

Teamwork is like an orchestra—when everyone plays their part in harmony, the result is beautiful. But when roles and responsibilities are unclear, you get chaos instead of a symphony.

Assigning roles and responsibilities is a crucial step in any project. It ensures accountability, keeps things moving, and helps the team work like a well-oiled machine. In this chapter, we'll dive into the art of understanding team dynamics, leveraging individual strengths, and creating a culture of ownership.

Why Roles and Responsibilities Matter

Imagine a soccer team where no one knows their position. The defenders try to score, the goalkeeper wanders into midfield, and chaos ensues. The same thing happens in projects when roles aren't clearly defined.

Assigning roles and responsibilities provides:

- **Clarity:** Everyone knows what's expected of them.
- **Efficiency:** Reduces duplicated efforts and missed tasks.
- **Accountability:** Ensures each team member takes ownership of their contributions.

Clear roles aren't just about efficiency—they're also about creating a sense of purpose and belonging.

Understanding Team Dynamics

Before assigning roles, it's essential to understand your team's dynamics. Who's good at what? Who prefers working behind the scenes, and who thrives in leadership roles?

Steps to Assess Team Dynamics:

1. **Observe Strengths:** Pay attention to what team members excel at. Is someone great at crunching numbers? Another at creative brainstorming?
2. **Ask Questions:** Have conversations with your team to understand their skills, interests, and preferences.
3. **Identify Gaps:** Recognize areas where additional support or skills might be needed.

Example:

For a product launch team:

- A tech-savvy teammate might handle digital tools.
- A creative thinker could lead branding and marketing.
- A detail-oriented person might manage logistics.

The Power of Accountability

Accountability doesn't mean micromanaging—it's about creating a culture where everyone feels responsible for the project's success. When team members know their roles and how they contribute to the bigger picture, they're more likely to stay motivated and engaged.

How to Foster Accountability:

1. **Set Clear Expectations:** Define what success looks like for each role.
2. **Empower Decision-Making:** Allow team members to take ownership of their tasks without constant oversight.

3. **Check-In Regularly:** Use updates and progress meetings to stay aligned without micromanaging.

Assigning Roles: The Right Person for the Right Task

Matching roles to strengths is like solving a puzzle—it's all about finding the perfect fit. Here's how to assign roles effectively:

1. Define the Roles Needed

List out all the tasks and responsibilities required for the project. For example:
- Project Coordinator: Oversees progress and keeps the team on track.
- Research Lead: Gathers and analyzes data.
- Communication Lead: Manages stakeholder updates.

2. Match Strengths to Roles

Assign roles based on each team member's skills, experience, and interests.

3. Clearly Communicate Responsibilities

Once roles are assigned, make sure everyone knows:
- What they're responsible for.
- Who they report to or collaborate with.
- How their role contributes to the project's success.

Example:

Task: Organizing a charity fundraiser.
- **Role:** Event Planner – Manages the venue and logistics.
- **Strength Needed:** Detail-oriented and organized.
- **Team Member Assigned:** Priya, who loves planning and has a track record of successful events.

Leveraging Strengths Within the Team

Every team member brings something unique to the table. By leveraging these strengths, you not only boost productivity but also create an environment where people feel valued and motivated.

Tips for Maximizing Strengths:
1. **Encourage Collaboration:** Pair team members with complementary skills. For example, a creative thinker can brainstorm ideas while a detail-oriented teammate refines them.
2. **Rotate Roles:** If possible, let team members try new roles to build their skills and keep things fresh.
3. **Celebrate Contributions:** Acknowledge individual and team achievements to boost morale.

Example:
In a software development project:
- A coder focuses on building the app.
- A user experience designer ensures it's easy to navigate.
- A project manager keeps everyone aligned and on schedule.

When everyone plays to their strengths, the project thrives.

Real-World Example: Success Through Teamwork

Let's look at a real-world example of clear roles driving success.

Scenario: A marketing team was tasked with creating a social media campaign in just two weeks. Instead of diving in haphazardly, the team:
- Assigned roles based on strengths (graphic design, content writing, scheduling).
- Clearly outlined responsibilities (e.g., "Amit will design 10 posts; Priya will write captions").
- Conducted daily check-ins to stay aligned.

The result? The campaign launched on time, exceeded engagement goals, and the team felt a shared sense of accomplishment.

Common Pitfalls (and How to Avoid Them)

Even with the best intentions, assigning roles can sometimes go wrong. Here's how to steer clear of trouble:

Pitfall: Overlapping Responsibilities

- **Solution:** Clearly define who owns each task.

Pitfall: Ignoring Individual Preferences

- **Solution:** Take the time to understand what motivates each team member.

Pitfall: Micromanaging

- **Solution:** Trust your team and focus on the bigger picture.

Final Thoughts: Building a Dream Team

Assigning roles and responsibilities isn't just about dividing tasks—it's about empowering your team to shine. When everyone knows their role and feels valued, the project becomes a shared journey toward success.

Remember:

- Understand team dynamics.
- Match roles to strengths.
- Foster a culture of accountability.

By mastering the art of role assignment, you're not just managing a project—you're building a team that's ready to tackle anything. Now, let's get your dream team in motion!

CHAPTER 12: TRACKING PROGRESS AND STAYING ORGANIZED

If a project is a journey, tracking progress is your GPS. Without it, you risk losing your way, running into unexpected roadblocks, or veering off course. Staying organized ensures you stay efficient, meet deadlines, and keep your team motivated. In this chapter, we'll explore the best tools for monitoring progress and practical strategies for tackling bottlenecks head-on.

Why Tracking Progress Matters

Imagine you're baking a cake without ever checking the recipe or peeking into the oven. You might end up with a masterpiece—or a burnt disaster. The same applies to projects. Tracking progress isn't about nitpicking—it's about ensuring every step contributes to the final goal.

Benefits of Monitoring Progress:

1. **Staying Aligned:** Keeps the team focused on the project's objectives.
2. **Spotting Issues Early:** Helps identify bottlenecks before they derail the project.
3. **Boosting Accountability:** Ensures everyone is on the same page about responsibilities.

4. **Building Momentum:** Regular check-ins create a sense of accomplishment.

The Best Tools for Monitoring Progress

Thankfully, you don't need to rely on sticky notes or scribbles in a notebook to track your project. Modern tools make staying organized easier than ever. Here's a quick overview of some popular options:

1. Trello

A visual, drag-and-drop tool that uses boards, lists, and cards to organize tasks.

- **Great For:** Simple projects, individual tasks, and team collaboration.
- **Pro Tip:** Use color-coded labels to categorize tasks by priority or phase.

2. Asana

A powerful tool for planning, organizing, and tracking work in one place.

- **Great For:** Complex projects with multiple teams.
- **Pro Tip:** Leverage the timeline feature to visualize deadlines and dependencies.

3. Microsoft Project

A robust tool designed for detailed project planning and tracking.

- **Great For:** Large-scale projects with intricate schedules.
- **Pro Tip:** Use the Gantt chart to monitor progress and adjust timelines dynamically.

4. Monday.com

A flexible platform that adapts to various workflows.

- **Great For:** Team collaboration and customizable task tracking.
- **Pro Tip:** Integrate with other tools like Slack or Google Drive for seamless coordination.

5. Google Sheets/Excel

Sometimes, simplicity is key. A well-structured spreadsheet can work wonders.

- **Great For:** Small projects or when you need quick customization.
- **Pro Tip:** Use conditional formatting to flag overdue tasks.

How to Stay Organized While Monitoring Progress

1. Establish Checkpoints

Break the project into milestones and review progress at each checkpoint.

- **Example:** For a product launch, checkpoints might include content creation, marketing rollout, and customer feedback.

2. Use Dashboards

Dashboards provide a bird's-eye view of the project's status, making it easy to spot what's on track and what's falling behind.

- **Tip:** Most tools like Asana or Monday.com offer built-in dashboards that you can customize.

3. Maintain a Task Tracker

Keep a master list of all tasks, assignees, and deadlines.

- **Example:** A Kanban board in Trello can visually represent what's in progress, done, or pending.

4. Regular Updates

Schedule short, frequent updates to ensure alignment without disrupting productivity.

- **Example:** A weekly 15-minute stand-up meeting can work wonders.

Identifying Bottlenecks: Where Projects Get Stuck

Even the best-laid plans can hit a snag. Bottlenecks—those points where progress slows or stops—are inevitable. The good news? They're manageable if addressed early.

Common Causes of Bottlenecks:
1. **Resource Constraints:** Not enough time, people, or tools.
2. **Communication Gaps:** Misunderstandings or delays in information sharing.
3. **Scope Creep:** When unplanned tasks pile onto the project.
4. **Decision Delays:** Waiting for approvals or key decisions.

How to Spot Bottlenecks Early

1. Analyze Task Completion Rates
Use your tracking tools to see if tasks are consistently falling behind schedule.
- **Example:** If a specific phase of the project lags, it might indicate a resource issue.

2. Monitor Workload Distribution
Check if any team member is overloaded or underutilized.
- **Tip:** Tools like Monday.com often include workload views to visualize team capacity.

3. Listen to Your Team
Encourage open communication about challenges. Your team often knows where bottlenecks are lurking.

4. Use Data Trends
Leverage analytics from your project management tools to identify patterns in delays or inefficiencies.

Breaking Through Bottlenecks
Once you've spotted a bottleneck, it's time to act:

1. Prioritize the Issue
Focus on resolving bottlenecks that have the most significant

impact on the project.

2. Reallocate Resources

Shift resources to the bottlenecked area, even temporarily, to ease the load.

3. Improve Communication

Create a clearer, faster communication channel for critical updates.

4. Reassess Deadlines

If delays are unavoidable, adjust timelines to ensure quality isn't compromised.

Example:

Bottleneck: A graphic designer is overwhelmed with tasks for a marketing campaign.
Solution:

- Reassign less-critical tasks to other team members.
- Use templates to speed up repetitive design work.

Real-World Example: Overcoming a Bottleneck

A tech startup was developing an app but faced delays during the testing phase. The bottleneck? Their sole tester was overwhelmed.

Solution:

- The team cross-trained developers to assist with basic testing.
- They streamlined the feedback process by using a centralized bug-tracking tool.

The result? The app launched on time, and the team learned how to work more flexibly for future projects.

Final Thoughts: Stay on Track, Stay Ahead

Tracking progress and staying organized are the keys to turning plans into reality. By embracing the right tools, staying proactive about bottlenecks, and fostering a culture of accountability, you can navigate any project confidently.

Remember:
- Use tools to lighten the load and bring clarity.
- Celebrate milestones to keep morale high.
- Tackle bottlenecks head-on to keep the project flowing smoothly.

When you master the art of tracking and organization, you'll not only deliver successful projects—you'll also lead your team to new heights of efficiency and achievement.

CHAPTER 13: REVIEW AND REFLECT: CLOSING THE PROJECT

Congratulations! The project is complete, the goals are met, and the finish line is behind you. But wait—don't rush off to the next thing just yet! Closing a project isn't just about popping the champagne (although that's a nice touch). It's about pausing, reflecting, and capturing the lessons learned so every future project can benefit from your newfound wisdom.

In this chapter, we'll dive into why the review process matters, how to make it meaningful, and what to document for long-term growth.

Why Closing a Project Matters

Imagine running a marathon and never checking your time or reflecting on how you trained. Sure, you finished, but how will you improve for the next race? Closing a project is like crossing the finish line with intention.

The Benefits of a Thorough Review:

1. **Celebrate Success:** Acknowledge what went well to boost team morale.
2. **Capture Lessons Learned:** Avoid repeating mistakes and replicate successes.
3. **Strengthen Skills:** Sharpen your project management toolkit for next time.

4. **Foster Growth:** Provide constructive feedback to team members and stakeholders.

Conducting a Project Review: The Essentials

A project review isn't about pointing fingers or assigning blame—it's about understanding what worked and what didn't. Here's how to make the process smooth and effective:

1. Gather Feedback

- **Who to Include:** Team members, stakeholders, and anyone significantly involved.
- **How to Collect It:** Use surveys, interviews, or casual team discussions.
- **Example Questions:**
    - What went well during the project?
    - What were the biggest challenges?
    - How could we improve the process next time?

2. Host a Lessons Learned Meeting

Bring everyone together for an open and honest discussion.

- **Structure the Meeting:**
    - **Start with Successes:** Highlight wins and milestones.
    - **Discuss Challenges:** Identify what caused delays or issues.
    - **Brainstorm Solutions:** Collaborate on ideas for improvement.

3. Evaluate Objectives vs. Outcomes

Compare what you planned to achieve with what you actually accomplished.

- **Questions to Ask:**
    - Did we meet the project's goals?
    - Were deadlines and budgets adhered to?

- Did the final deliverables meet expectations?

4. Assess Team Dynamics

Review how the team functioned as a unit.

- **Key Areas to Evaluate:**
    - Communication: Were updates timely and clear?
    - Collaboration: Did team members support one another effectively?
    - Roles: Were responsibilities well-defined?

Documenting Successes and Areas for Improvement

Once the review is complete, it's time to put pen to paper (or fingers to keyboard). A project without documentation is like a great meal without a recipe—hard to replicate.

1. Create a Final Report

Summarize the project's journey, from initiation to closure. Include:

- Key milestones
- Budget and timeline adherence
- Deliverables achieved

2. Write a Lessons Learned Log

Capture insights to guide future projects.

- **Format:** A simple table works well.
    - **Column 1:** What went well?
    - **Column 2:** What didn't work?
    - **Column 3:** Recommendations for next time.

3. Highlight Success Stories

Document the standout moments and contributions from your team.

- **Example:** "Our marketing team exceeded expectations, generating 30% more leads than forecasted."

4. Organize Files for Future Reference

Ensure all documents, reports, and assets are stored in a centralized location.

> **Tip:** Use cloud-based tools like Google Drive or SharePoint for easy access.

Real-World Example: Reflecting for Growth

When a small nonprofit organization completed its annual fundraising campaign, they realized their donor engagement had skyrocketed compared to the previous year. During their project review, they identified two key successes:

1. Personalized email outreach resonated deeply with donors.
2. Weekly team check-ins kept everyone aligned.

However, they also noted a challenge: their initial timeline was too tight, causing unnecessary stress.

Outcome:

For the next campaign, they decided to start planning earlier and replicate their personalized email strategy. The result? Even greater success the following year.

Tips for a Successful Review Process

1. **Keep It Constructive:** Focus on growth, not criticism.
2. **Encourage Openness:** Create a safe space for honest feedback.
3. **Be Timely:** Conduct reviews shortly after project completion while details are fresh.
4. **Involve Everyone:** Each voice matters, from interns to executives.

Celebrate and Move Forward

Closing a project is also about celebration. Recognize the hard work, perseverance, and creativity that brought it to life. Whether it's a team lunch, a shoutout in a company meeting, or a simple thank-you email, acknowledging effort goes a long way.

Final Takeaways:
- A thorough review turns a project into a stepping stone for growth.
- Documenting lessons learned ensures continuous improvement.
- Celebrating success fosters a positive team culture.

As you wrap up this chapter—and your next project—remember: every ending is a new beginning. With every reflection, you're not just closing a chapter; you're writing the prologue to your next success story.

PART 4: TOOLS, TEMPLATES, AND TECHNIQUES

CHAPTER 14: THE POWER OF PROJECT MANAGEMENT TOOLS

Imagine trying to build a house without the right tools—hammering nails with a rock or measuring wood with a guess. Frustrating, right? The same applies to managing projects. Without the proper tools, even the simplest tasks can feel overwhelming. Thankfully, project management tools are like the Swiss Army knives of productivity—they make organizing, tracking, and collaborating a breeze.

In this chapter, we'll explore some of the most popular tools, uncover what makes them tick, and help you choose the one that fits your unique needs.

Why Project Management Tools Matter

Whether you're managing a major project or just coordinating a few tasks, tools can make the process smoother.

What They Do:
- **Organize Chaos:** Keep tasks, timelines, and responsibilities in one place.
- **Boost Collaboration:** Ensure team members stay on the same page.
- **Track Progress:** Monitor deadlines and milestones effortlessly.
- **Save Time:** Automate repetitive tasks, like sending

reminders or updating schedules.

Meet the Stars: Popular Project Management Tools

Let's introduce some of the heavyweights in the project management world.

1. Trello: Visual and User-Friendly

- **Best For:** Simpler projects, visual thinkers, small teams.
- **Features:**
  - Drag-and-drop boards for tasks.
  - Color-coded labels for priorities.
  - Checklists within tasks to track sub-tasks.
- **Why People Love It:** Trello's clean, intuitive design makes it perfect for beginners and non-technical users.

2. Asana: Collaboration King

- **Best For:** Teams juggling multiple projects, task-heavy workflows.
- **Features:**
  - Task assignments with deadlines.
  - Project timelines for long-term planning.
  - Integration with tools like Slack and Google Drive.
- **Why People Love It:** Asana shines in fostering teamwork and breaking down complex projects into manageable steps.

3. Microsoft Project: The Powerhouse

- **Best For:** Large-scale, detailed projects, experienced project managers.
- **Features:**
  - Advanced Gantt charts for timelines.
  - Budget tracking to monitor costs.
  - Resource allocation to optimize team efforts.

- **Why People Love It:** If you need a tool with robust functionality and detailed reporting, Microsoft Project delivers.

How to Select the Right Tool for Your Needs

With so many options, how do you pick the perfect fit? It's all about understanding your requirements.

Step 1: Identify Your Goals

- Are you managing simple to-do lists or complex, multi-phase projects?
- Do you need collaboration features for a team or a solo solution?

Step 2: Consider Your Workflow

- Do you prefer visual layouts like Trello's boards, or do you need detailed timelines like Microsoft Project?
- Is flexibility important, or do you need a structured approach?

Step 3: Factor in Team Size and Skill Level

- For small teams or beginners, tools like Trello are ideal.
- For larger, experienced teams, Asana or Microsoft Project may be a better fit.

Step 4: Budget Matters

- Free options: Trello's basic plan, Asana's free tier.
- Paid plans: Advanced features in Asana or Microsoft Project come at a cost but offer more power.

Real-World Example: Choosing the Right Tool

When a mid-sized marketing agency began juggling multiple campaigns, they struggled with task overlap and missed deadlines. Initially, they tried Trello for its simplicity, but as their needs grew, they transitioned to Asana to handle increased complexity.

Outcome:
With Asana, they streamlined communication, tracked tasks in real-time, and reduced project delays by 30%. The key was starting simple and scaling up as their requirements evolved.

Tips for Getting Started with Project Management Tools

1. **Start Small:** Begin with a single project to get comfortable.
2. **Leverage Tutorials:** Most tools offer free resources to help you learn the ropes.
3. **Customize for Your Needs:** Adjust settings, templates, and layouts to suit your style.
4. **Encourage Team Adoption:** Share benefits with your team to ensure everyone's onboard.
5. **Experiment:** Try free trials of several tools to see which feels right.

The Future of Project Management Tools

As technology evolves, project management tools are becoming smarter. From AI-driven scheduling to real-time progress analytics, the possibilities are endless. By adopting the right tools today, you're not just simplifying your projects—you're preparing for the future of work.

Final Takeaway

The right project management tool isn't just a nice-to-have; it's a game-changer. It transforms how you organize, communicate, and execute. Whether you're mapping out a massive project or just managing your daily tasks, there's a tool out there waiting to make your life easier.

Remember: The tool is just that—a tool. It's how you use it that makes all the difference. So, explore, experiment, and unleash the power of project management tools to organize and excel like

GITANGSHU ADHIKARY

never before!

CHAPTER 15: TEMPLATES AND CHECKLISTS: SIMPLIFYING YOUR WORKFLOW

Picture this: you're about to start a big project, and instead of staring at a blank page or wrangling a chaotic task list, you have a ready-made structure waiting for you. Sounds amazing, right? That's the magic of templates and checklists. They're your cheat codes for simplifying your workflow, saving time, and ensuring nothing slips through the cracks.

Let's dive into why templates and checklists are a must-have for any project and how you can make them work for you.

Why Templates and Checklists Matter

Templates and checklists are like your project's GPS. They:

- **Provide Direction:** Offer a clear starting point so you're not reinventing the wheel.
- **Ensure Consistency:** Keep processes uniform, especially across teams.
- **Save Time:** Cut down the prep work so you can focus on execution.
- **Prevent Oversights:** With a checklist, nothing gets

forgotten—ever.

Whether you're managing a team presentation, launching a product, or organizing a personal event, having the right template or checklist can make all the difference.

Essential Project Templates You Can't Live Without

Here are some go-to templates that can make your workflow a breeze:

1. Project Charter Template

- **What It Does:** Outlines project objectives, scope, and key stakeholders.
- **Why It's Useful:** Sets the foundation for every project by clarifying the "why" and "what."
- **Example Sections:**
  - Project Purpose
  - Goals and Deliverables
  - Stakeholders and Roles

2. Task Tracker Template

- **What It Does:** Helps you assign tasks, set deadlines, and monitor progress.
- **Why It's Useful:** Keeps everyone accountable and tasks visible.
- **Example Columns:**
  - Task Name
  - Assigned To
  - Priority (High, Medium, Low)
  - Status (To Do, In Progress, Done)

3. Risk Assessment Template

- **What It Does:** Identifies potential risks and plans for mitigation.
- **Why It's Useful:** Helps you foresee challenges before they arise.

- **Example Fields:**
  - Risk Description
  - Impact Level (Low, Medium, High)
  - Mitigation Plan

4. **Meeting Agenda Template**
   - **What It Does:** Structures your meetings for maximum productivity.
   - **Why It's Useful:** Keeps discussions focused and action-driven.
   - **Example Sections:**
     - Meeting Objective
     - Key Discussion Points
     - Action Items

5. **Post-Project Review Template**
   - **What It Does:** Guides your team through evaluating what worked and what didn't.
   - **Why It's Useful:** Provides insights for future improvements.
   - **Example Sections:**
     - Successes and Wins
     - Challenges Faced
     - Lessons Learned

The Power of Checklists

Checklists are the unsung heroes of project management. They're simple yet incredibly effective at keeping you on track. Here's how they can help:

1. **Break Down Complex Tasks:** Turn overwhelming projects into bite-sized steps.
2. **Maintain Focus:** Highlight what's done and what's left.
3. **Boost Confidence:** There's nothing more satisfying than

ticking off a completed task!

Example Checklist: Preparing for a Team Presentation
- Define the objective of the presentation.
- Create a slide deck and rehearse.
- Assign roles (who presents what).
- Set up the tech (projector, laptop, etc.).
- Conduct a final review and dry run.

Customizing Templates and Checklists for Your Needs

One size doesn't fit all. Here's how to make templates and checklists work specifically for you:

1. Identify Your Workflow
- Look at your past projects: What steps did you follow? Where did things go wrong?
- Use these insights to tweak templates to fit your needs.

2. Personalize for Your Industry
- Are you in marketing? Add campaign timelines to your templates.
- Working in software? Include sprint planning and testing phases.

3. Keep It Simple
- Don't overcomplicate. Start with the essentials and add details as needed.

4. Update Regularly
- Review your templates and checklists after each project.
- Make adjustments to improve efficiency for next time.

Real-Life Example: A Checklist That Saved the Day

Consider Priya, a non-project manager tasked with organizing her company's annual client meeting. She used a meeting agenda template to plan every detail—from booking the venue to assigning presentation topics. She also created a checklist to

ensure no stone was left unturned:
- Confirm venue availability ✓
- Send calendar invites ✓
- Prepare welcome kits for attendees ✓
- Arrange catering services ✓

The result? The meeting went off without a hitch, and Priya received glowing feedback for her flawless organization.

Tips for Making the Most of Templates and Checklists

1. **Use Tools:** Platforms like Trello, Asana, or Notion often include ready-to-use templates.
2. **Collaborate:** Share templates with your team to ensure everyone's aligned.
3. **Automate:** Many tools allow you to duplicate templates, saving even more time.
4. **Start Small:** Begin with one or two templates and build as your needs grow.

Final Thoughts

Templates and checklists are your secret weapons for conquering chaos and keeping projects on track. They're more than just time-savers—they're stress-reducers and efficiency boosters.

So why not start today? Whether you're planning a team project or your next family vacation, grab a template, whip up a checklist, and watch your workflow transform into a well-oiled machine.

Remember, simplicity is the ultimate sophistication. With the right templates and checklists, you'll not only simplify your work—you'll elevate it!

CHAPTER 16: EFFECTIVE COMMUNICATION IN PROJECT MANAGEMENT

Communication can make or break a project. Imagine a game of telephone gone wrong—messages get muddled, expectations misaligned, and before you know it, confusion reigns. On the flip side, clear, concise communication acts like a GPS for your team, ensuring everyone is on the same page and heading toward the same destination.

This chapter unpacks the strategies that make project communication not just effective but impactful. Ready to master the art of keeping everyone informed, aligned, and motivated? Let's dive in!

The Role of Communication in Project Success

Think of communication as the glue holding your project together. It connects:

- **The Big Picture to the Details:** Ensures everyone understands the overall goals and their role in achieving them.
- **Teams and Stakeholders:** Keeps everyone informed,

involved, and engaged.
- **Problems to Solutions:** Facilitates quick identification and resolution of issues before they snowball.

Without strong communication, even the best-laid plans can unravel.

Strategies for Clear and Concise Communication

Mastering communication doesn't require a degree in public speaking—it's about adopting a few practical strategies:

1. Start with the End in Mind
- **Define Your Purpose:** Why are you communicating? To inform, clarify, or get feedback?
- **Tailor Your Message:** Adjust your language, tone, and detail level for your audience. Stakeholders might need big-picture updates, while team members need specific instructions.

2. Keep It Simple and Focused
- **Avoid Jargon:** Use straightforward language, especially when addressing mixed audiences.
- **Stick to the Point:** Highlight the most critical information to avoid overwhelming your audience.
- **Be Structured:** Use formats like bullet points or numbered lists for clarity.

3. Choose the Right Medium
Different messages call for different communication channels:
- **Email:** For detailed updates or documentation.
- **Meetings:** For brainstorming, problem-solving, or high-priority updates.
- **Messaging Apps (Slack, Teams):** For quick questions or informal updates.
- **Dashboards/Reports:** For sharing data-driven progress.

4. Make It Two-Way

- **Invite Feedback:** Encourage questions and input to ensure everyone is on the same page.
- **Listen Actively:** Pay attention to what's being said—and what's not. Silence can be as telling as words.

Managing Expectations with Stakeholders

Stakeholders—whether clients, team members, or higher-ups—play a pivotal role in project success. Managing their expectations is part art, part science, and all about communication.

1. Set Expectations Early
- **Define Deliverables:** Clarify what the project will—and won't—achieve.
- **Agree on Milestones:** Ensure everyone is aligned on timelines and outcomes.

2. Communicate Regularly
- **Status Updates:** Keep stakeholders informed with consistent updates, whether weekly emails or bi-monthly meetings.
- **Be Transparent:** Share successes and challenges alike. Honesty builds trust.

3. Handle Changes Gracefully
- **Acknowledge Concerns:** If priorities shift or obstacles arise, address them head-on.
- **Propose Solutions:** Frame changes as opportunities for improvement.

Practical Tools for Better Communication

Maximize your communication efforts with tools that streamline the process:

1. Project Management Software

Platforms like Trello, Asana, or Monday.com offer built-in communication features that keep everyone connected.

- Assign tasks and tag team members for clarity.
- Centralize conversations to avoid email overload.

2. Collaborative Document Tools

Google Docs, Microsoft Teams, or Notion allow real-time updates and comments, fostering collaboration and reducing misunderstandings.

3. Video Conferencing

For remote teams, tools like Zoom or Microsoft Teams ensure face-to-face interaction when it matters most.

Real-World Communication Wins

Case 1: The Weekly Check-In Saves the Day

Imagine a marketing team working on a product launch. By implementing a 15-minute weekly check-in, they noticed small hiccups early—like overlapping deadlines or unclear roles. These quick conversations saved time and reduced stress, ensuring a seamless launch.

Case 2: Stakeholder Alignment Avoids Disaster

A software development team faced mid-project scope changes from a key client. Regular stakeholder meetings helped the team stay agile, adjust priorities, and deliver a product that exceeded expectations—all without last-minute surprises.

Final Thoughts

Effective communication isn't just a skill—it's the backbone of successful project management. By keeping your messages clear, choosing the right tools, and fostering open dialogue, you'll ensure smoother workflows, happier teams, and projects that hit the mark.

So, start small: send that concise email, schedule that quick check-in, or refine your project update process. Remember, great communication is the secret sauce that turns good projects into great ones!

PART 5: APPLYING PROJECT MANAGEMENT PRINCIPLES IN EVERYDAY WORK

CHAPTER 17: PROJECT MANAGEMENT FOR PERSONAL TASKS

Ever felt like you're juggling a million things, only to drop a few along the way? Whether it's managing a work deadline, planning a family vacation, or even tackling a home renovation, life throws projects at us daily. Here's the secret: project management isn't just for the workplace—it's a game-changer for personal tasks too.

This chapter will show you how to harness project management techniques to organize your life, reduce stress, and accomplish your goals with finesse. Let's turn your to-do list into a done list!

Organizing Complex Tasks at Work

Even if you don't have the title "Project Manager," you're already managing projects in your daily work. Think about that client presentation, cross-departmental collaboration, or event planning—it's all project management in disguise.

Step 1: Define Your Objective

What are you trying to achieve? Be crystal clear about the end goal. For instance:

- Instead of "Prepare a presentation," aim for "Deliver a 30-minute client pitch with compelling visuals and actionable insights."

Step 2: Break It Down

Large tasks can feel overwhelming. Break them into manageable

steps:
1. Research and gather data.
2. Draft the outline.
3. Create slides.
4. Practice the delivery.

Each step is a mini-task, and completing them will give you a sense of progress and momentum.

Step 3: Prioritize and Plan

Some steps are more urgent than others. Rank them by importance and deadlines. Use tools like:
- **Checklists:** For a simple approach.
- **Kanban Boards (e.g., Trello):** To visualize progress.
- **Calendar Blocking:** To allocate time for each step.

Step 4: Collaborate Effectively

If your task involves others, assign clear responsibilities. Be specific about who's doing what and when, ensuring accountability and reducing last-minute chaos.

Applying PM Skills to Personal Goals

Your personal life deserves the same level of care and planning as your professional projects. Here's how project management can help you nail your personal goals.

Scenario 1: Planning a Vacation

A dream trip can quickly turn into a nightmare without proper planning. Here's how to PM your getaway:

1. **Initiation:** Set a clear goal (e.g., "Spend a week in Bali exploring beaches, temples, and local cuisine within a $2,000 budget").
2. **Planning:** Create a checklist of tasks—booking flights, reserving accommodations, researching activities, and budgeting.
3. **Execution:** Tackle each task step by step, involving travel

companions for shared responsibilities.
4. **Monitoring:** Keep an eye on timelines (e.g., early-bird discounts) and adjust plans if necessary.
5. **Closure:** Enjoy the trip, take notes for future planning, and reflect on what worked well!

Scenario 2: Tackling a Home Renovation

Renovations often go over budget and schedule. Avoid this with PM principles:

1. **Define the Scope:** What areas will you renovate, and what's the desired outcome?
2. **Create a Budget and Timeline:** Be realistic and include buffers for unexpected costs or delays.
3. **Assign Roles:** DIY tasks vs. hiring professionals.
4. **Monitor Progress:** Use tools like a shared spreadsheet to track expenses and milestones.

Scenario 3: Achieving Personal Goals

Want to write a novel, learn a language, or run a marathon? Treat it like a project:

- **Set SMART Goals:** Specific, Measurable, Achievable, Relevant, and Time-bound.
- **Plan Phases:** Break the goal into steps. For a marathon, this could be: training plan, nutrition, and gear preparation.
- **Track Progress:** Use apps like Strava (for fitness) or Duolingo (for languages) to stay motivated.

Tips for Success

1. **Visualize Your Goal:** Create a vision board or use digital tools to keep the outcome in sight.
2. **Celebrate Milestones:** Acknowledge small wins to stay motivated.
3. **Be Flexible:** Life happens—adapt your plan without

losing sight of the big picture.
4. **Seek Help:** Don't hesitate to involve others, whether it's delegating chores or asking for advice.

Real-Life Stories of PM at Home

Meet Priya: The Efficient Parent

Priya, a working mom, uses project management to organize her kids' school events and extracurricular activities. By creating a shared calendar and assigning responsibilities to her spouse and kids, she avoids last-minute scrambles and finds more time for herself.

Meet Ankit: The Budget-Savvy Traveler

Ankit planned a solo Europe trip with PM techniques. He mapped out an itinerary, tracked expenses in a spreadsheet, and used a Kanban app to organize visa applications and bookings. Result? A stress-free adventure under budget!

Final Thoughts

Project management isn't just a skill—it's a mindset. By applying its principles to your personal tasks, you can transform chaos into clarity and achieve more with less stress.

So, the next time you're faced with a daunting task—at work or home—remember: break it down, plan it out, and tackle it like a pro.

CHAPTER 18: HANDLING MULTIPLE PROJECTS WITHOUT THE OVERWHELM

Have you ever felt like you're spinning plates, with each one threatening to come crashing down? Managing multiple projects —whether at work or in life—can feel overwhelming. But here's the good news: with the right strategies, you can juggle priorities effectively and keep those plates spinning like a pro.

This chapter is your toolkit for staying on top of multiple projects without losing your cool. Let's dive into how you can master the art of multitasking while maintaining your sanity.

The Multitasking Myth: Why Prioritization is Key

First things first: multitasking doesn't mean doing everything at once. It's about managing your energy and focus across multiple priorities. The key to success is prioritization—not perfection.

When you have several projects demanding your attention, ask yourself:

1. **What's most urgent?** Deadlines are non-negotiable.
2. **What's most important?** Even without a tight deadline, some tasks have long-term value.
3. **What can wait?** Not everything needs immediate attention.

By categorizing your projects this way, you can tackle the most critical tasks first without feeling pulled in a million directions.

Strategies for Juggling Multiple Priorities

1. Plan Your Week in Advance

Every Sunday or Monday morning, set aside time to plan your week. Use tools like:

- **Calendars** to block time for specific projects.
- **To-Do Lists** to outline daily priorities.
- **Project Boards (e.g., Trello or Asana)** to visualize progress across multiple projects.

Pro tip: Start with the tasks that require the most focus and energy, tackling them when you're freshest (usually in the morning).

2. Embrace the "Two-Minute Rule"

For small, quick tasks, follow this golden rule: if it takes less than two minutes, do it now. Clearing these minor items off your plate keeps your list manageable and reduces mental clutter.

3. Group Similar Tasks Together

Switching contexts repeatedly wastes time and energy. Instead, batch similar tasks:

- Answer all emails in one focused session.
- Schedule meetings back-to-back to keep your day free for deep work.
- Complete all brainstorming or creative tasks in one stretch.

4. Delegate Where Possible

Remember, you don't have to do everything yourself. Delegate tasks to team members, colleagues, or even tools. Not only does this free up your time, but it also empowers others to contribute.

Time Management Tips for Non-Project Managers

1. Use the 80/20 Rule

The Pareto Principle states that 80% of results come from 20% of your efforts. Focus on the few tasks that make the biggest impact on your projects.

2. Block Time for Focused Work

Set aside uninterrupted blocks of time for your most important projects. Silence notifications, close unnecessary tabs, and create a distraction-free zone.

3. Build in Buffers

Life is unpredictable. Add buffer time between tasks or projects to accommodate delays, emergencies, or simply to recharge.

4. Learn to Say No

It's okay to decline new projects if your plate is already full. Saying no doesn't mean you're unhelpful—it shows you value quality over quantity.

Real-World Examples: Managing the Chaos Like a Pro

Ravi: The Team Player

Ravi works in a small team and often juggles multiple responsibilities. He uses a simple prioritization system:

- **Red Tasks:** Urgent and important (do first).
- **Yellow Tasks:** Important but not urgent (schedule).
- **Green Tasks:** Neither urgent nor important (delegate or defer).

This approach keeps him organized and ensures nothing falls through the cracks.

Meera: The Multitasking Mom

Meera manages her job, her kids' school schedules, and a small side business. She uses time blocking to allocate focused periods for work, family, and self-care. By planning her day the night before, she wakes up feeling prepared rather than overwhelmed.

Your Action Plan for Juggling Projects

1. **List Your Projects:** Write down everything you're working on.
2. **Prioritize:** Sort them by urgency and importance.
3. **Create a Weekly Schedule:** Plan your tasks and block time for each project.
4. **Use Tools:** Experiment with apps like Trello, Asana, or even a physical planner.
5. **Review and Adjust:** At the end of each week, evaluate what worked and tweak your plan for the next.

Final Thoughts

Juggling multiple projects doesn't have to be a source of stress. With a clear strategy and the right tools, you can transform chaos into calm and get everything done without feeling overwhelmed.

Remember: You're not just managing projects—you're mastering them. Stay focused, stay flexible, and keep moving forward.

CHAPTER 19: COLLABORATION ACROSS TEAMS AND DEPARTMENTS

Imagine a symphony orchestra, where every musician plays their part in harmony to create a beautiful performance. Now picture the chaos if each section ignored the conductor or played their own tune. Cross-team collaboration in the workplace is a lot like that symphony—when teams work together, magic happens. But when silos form, progress comes to a screeching halt.

This chapter is your guide to breaking down barriers, improving cross-functional collaboration, and aligning objectives for collective success. Ready to turn workplace silos into symphonies? Let's go!

The Problem with Silos

Silos happen when teams or departments work in isolation, hoarding information or pursuing goals that don't align with the bigger picture. While this isn't always intentional, it can:

- Slow down progress due to duplication of effort.
- Lead to miscommunication or mistrust.
- Create conflicting priorities that undermine overall success.

Breaking silos requires a mindset shift from "my team" to "our organization." Collaboration doesn't just make work smoother—it amplifies innovation, speeds up solutions, and ensures everyone's efforts are aligned.

Building Bridges: Strategies for Better Collaboration

1. Open Communication Channels

The foundation of collaboration is communication. Teams can't work together if they don't talk to each other. Foster open, transparent communication with tools like:

- **Slack or Microsoft Teams:** Perfect for quick, ongoing conversations.
- **Shared Dashboards (e.g., Trello, Asana):** Keep everyone updated on progress and deadlines.
- **Regular Check-ins:** Weekly or bi-weekly meetings to align goals and address roadblocks.

Pro tip: Always include a mix of real-time (meetings, calls) and asynchronous (emails, project boards) communication to accommodate different work styles.

2. Establish Clear Objectives

Confusion kills collaboration. Make sure everyone understands:

- **The overarching goal:** Why this project matters to the organization.
- **Individual roles:** Who's responsible for what.
- **Interdependencies:** How one team's work impacts another's success.

Creating a shared sense of purpose ensures every team pulls in the same direction.

3. Foster Empathy Between Teams

Encourage teams to see the world through each other's eyes. For example:

- **Sales Teams:** Understand the time and effort required for product development.

- **Product Teams:** Recognize the challenges of meeting customer expectations in real-time.

Empathy builds respect, and respect fosters smoother collaboration.

4. Celebrate Wins—Together

When collaboration leads to success, share the credit. Publicly acknowledge contributions from all teams involved. Recognition motivates teams to continue working together.

Aligning Objectives for Collective Success

Even the best collaboration efforts fail without aligned goals. Here's how to get everyone on the same page:

1. Start with a Shared Vision

Kick off cross-departmental projects by defining a unified vision. For example:

- **What's the ultimate outcome?**
- **How will success be measured?**
- **What are the key milestones?**

A shared vision acts as a compass, guiding all teams toward the same destination.

2. Use SMART Goals

Break the vision into Specific, Measurable, Achievable, Relevant, and Time-bound goals. Assign these goals to individual teams while ensuring they're interconnected.

3. Regularly Revisit Objectives

Business priorities change, and so do project goals. Regularly check in with all teams to ensure objectives are still aligned. If adjustments are needed, communicate them clearly and quickly.

Real-World Examples of Cross-Team Collaboration

Example 1: Marketing Meets Product Development

A tech company wanted to launch a new app. The marketing team gathered user feedback through surveys, while the product team turned those insights into features. Weekly alignment meetings ensured both teams worked in lockstep, resulting in a successful launch and rave customer reviews.

Example 2: HR and IT Join Forces

During a company-wide software transition, the HR team trained employees on the new system, while IT handled technical support. By aligning their efforts, they reduced downtime and ensured a smooth transition for everyone.

Collaboration in Action: Your Roadmap

Here's how to put these strategies into practice:

1. **Initiate Cross-Team Discussions:** Start the conversation about goals and roles early.
2. **Use Collaboration Tools:** Experiment with platforms that streamline teamwork.
3. **Foster a Collaborative Culture:** Encourage openness, empathy, and recognition.
4. **Measure and Reflect:** Track the success of collaborative efforts and identify areas for improvement.

The Big Picture

Collaboration across teams and departments isn't just a nice-to-have—it's a must-have for organizational success. By breaking down silos and aligning objectives, you create an environment where ideas flow freely, innovation thrives, and everyone feels connected to a greater purpose.

Remember: the best results come when we work together. Whether you're tackling a complex project or addressing everyday challenges, collaboration turns individual efforts into collective triumphs. Now go build those bridges!

PART 6: MOVING FORWARD

CHAPTER 20: COMMON PITFALLS AND HOW TO AVOID THEM

Let's face it—no project goes perfectly from start to finish. Even the most experienced project managers hit bumps in the road. For non-project managers, the challenges can feel even more overwhelming. But here's the good news: every pitfall is an opportunity to grow, adapt, and improve.

In this chapter, we'll dive into common hurdles non-project managers face and, more importantly, how to overcome them with confidence. Ready to turn setbacks into stepping stones? Let's go!

Pitfall #1: Vague Goals and Objectives

The Problem:

Without clear goals, projects can drift aimlessly, leaving everyone confused about what success looks like. Imagine planning a trip without deciding the destination—you'll waste time, energy, and resources.

The Solution:

Start by defining **SMART goals** (Specific, Measurable, Achievable, Relevant, Time-bound). For example:

- Instead of saying, "Improve customer satisfaction," set a

goal like, "Increase positive customer feedback by 15% within three months."

Regularly revisit these goals with your team to ensure everyone stays aligned.

Pitfall #2: Poor Time Management
The Problem:

Deadlines sneak up, tasks pile up, and suddenly you're scrambling to catch up. Sound familiar? Poor time management can derail even the best-laid plans.

The Solution:
1. **Prioritize Tasks:** Use tools like the Eisenhower Matrix to categorize tasks into urgent/important quadrants.
2. **Break It Down:** Divide big projects into smaller, manageable chunks with clear deadlines.
3. **Set Buffers:** Always allocate extra time for unexpected delays—it's your safety net.

Remember, time management isn't about doing everything at once. It's about doing the right things at the right time.

Pitfall #3: Ineffective Communication
The Problem:

Miscommunication leads to misunderstandings, missed deadlines, and frustration. It's like playing a game of telephone—what you say isn't always what others hear.

The Solution:
1. **Be Clear and Concise:** Avoid jargon and stick to plain language, especially when explaining complex ideas.
2. **Choose the Right Medium:** Use emails for formal updates, instant messaging for quick clarifications, and meetings for detailed discussions.
3. **Encourage Feedback:** Always ask, "Does this make sense?" or "Do you have any questions?" to ensure

everyone is on the same page.

Pro tip: Document key decisions and share them with the team to avoid confusion later.

Pitfall #4: Overcommitment

The Problem:

Taking on too much at once can stretch resources thin and leave you—and your team—feeling overwhelmed.

The Solution:

1. **Learn to Say No:** Politely decline tasks that don't align with project priorities.
2. **Delegate Wisely:** Trust your team to handle tasks they're equipped for. Delegation isn't a sign of weakness; it's a hallmark of strong leadership.
3. **Focus on Impact:** Concentrate on tasks that deliver the most value, and let go of the rest.

Pitfall #5: Resistance to Change

The Problem:

Change is uncomfortable, and it's easy to resist new methods, tools, or processes. But clinging to "the way we've always done it" can hold your project back.

The Solution:

1. **Embrace Flexibility:** Be open to adapting plans as circumstances evolve.
2. **Involve the Team:** Get input from team members when introducing changes. People are more likely to support what they help create.
3. **Focus on Benefits:** Frame changes in terms of the positive outcomes they'll bring, like saving time or improving results.

Turning Setbacks into Learning Opportunities

Every project has its share of hiccups. The key is to view challenges not as failures, but as valuable lessons. Here's how:

1. **Conduct a Post-Mortem:** After a project ends, gather the team to discuss what went well and what didn't. Focus on solutions rather than blame.
2. **Keep a Lessons Learned Log:** Document insights from each project to avoid repeating mistakes in the future.
3. **Celebrate Progress:** Even if things didn't go perfectly, acknowledge the effort and accomplishments along the way.

Real-World Example: Learning from Mistakes

Imagine this scenario: A small business owner launches a marketing campaign but forgets to set a clear deadline for content creation. As the launch date approaches, panic sets in.

What They Did:

- They paused to regroup, setting a clear timeline and assigning specific tasks.
- They debriefed the team afterward, identifying the need for better planning in future campaigns.

The Outcome:
The campaign launched a week late but was ultimately a success. The team learned the importance of upfront planning and improved their process for the next project.

Final Thoughts

Mistakes and setbacks are inevitable, but they're also invaluable. Each one teaches you something new about managing projects and working with people. The key is to approach challenges with curiosity, resilience, and a commitment to improvement.

Remember, even seasoned professionals started as beginners. The fact that you're learning, adapting, and growing means you're already on the path to success. So embrace the journey—pitfalls and all—and keep moving forward.

CHAPTER 21: BECOMING A PROJECT MANAGEMENT ADVOCATE

You've learned the fundamentals of project management, honed key skills, and seen firsthand how they can make a difference. Now, it's time to take things a step further: becoming a Project Management (PM) advocate. Imagine this: you're not just applying PM techniques in your own work, but you're helping to spread the word, encouraging others to embrace these powerful tools.

In this chapter, we're going to talk about how to share your PM knowledge with others and use your skills to influence positive change in your organization. Ready to become the PM champion your team needs? Let's get started!

Why Advocacy Matters

You've already experienced how powerful project management can be in improving efficiency, reducing stress, and driving better results. But the impact doesn't stop with you! When you share your knowledge and encourage others to embrace PM practices, you're contributing to the long-term success of your organization.

When PM principles are applied across departments, teams, and individuals, the benefits multiply:

- **Better coordination** across teams

- **Fewer missed deadlines** and clearer priorities
- **More effective use of resources** and reduced waste

By advocating for PM, you're helping to create a culture of accountability, collaboration, and continuous improvement. And who wouldn't want to be a part of that?

Step 1: Start with Yourself—Become the Role Model

Before you start sharing your PM knowledge, make sure you're walking the talk. The best way to inspire others is by leading through example. Here's how:

1. **Use PM Tools and Techniques:**
   - Show how using a simple tool like Trello or Asana has helped you stay organized. Share your success stories of how breaking a large task into smaller phases improved your efficiency.
   - Mention how you handle deadlines by setting clear priorities and working with others to adjust expectations when needed.
2. **Demonstrate Effective Communication:**
   - Highlight how you've effectively communicated project goals, timelines, and potential obstacles with stakeholders.
   - Show how keeping an open line of communication reduces confusion and keeps the team aligned.
3. **Celebrate Small Wins:**
   - Share your accomplishments—big or small. Show how planning, setting goals, and tracking progress led to success. When others see the tangible benefits of PM in your work, they'll be more likely to give it a try themselves.

Step 2: Share Knowledge in Casual Conversations

You don't need to give a full-fledged presentation to start sharing PM practices. Begin with small conversations. Over time, these casual discussions can spark greater interest and build momentum.

Here's how you can weave PM concepts into everyday conversations:

- "Did you know how much time we could save if we used a task tracker like Asana for that?"
- "We might be able to finish this earlier if we break it down into smaller steps, like we do in project management."
- "I just started planning my work with clearer deadlines, and it's been a game-changer. I get things done faster and with less stress."

These small comments can plant the seeds for others to become interested in PM techniques. When people see how PM practices positively affect your work, they'll start wondering how they can benefit too!

Step 3: Host PM Training Sessions or Workshops

When the time is right, consider hosting short training sessions or workshops to share your knowledge more formally. Don't worry if you're not a professional trainer—you're simply sharing what you know. The goal is to create an interactive and fun environment that inspires others to take action.

Here are a few ways to structure these sessions:

1. **Focus on Practical Tips:**
   Share easy-to-implement PM techniques. For example, walk through creating a basic project plan or how to prioritize tasks using simple tools.
2. **Use Real Examples:**
   If possible, bring in real projects (or examples from

your own work) to demonstrate how PM practices can improve project success. People are more likely to connect with something they can see in action.

3. **Interactive Exercises:**
   Encourage people to actively participate. Have them break a fictional project into phases, prioritize tasks, or brainstorm potential risks. The hands-on approach will make PM concepts stick.

4. **Keep It Short and Sweet:**
   No need to make it a full-day seminar—keep your sessions bite-sized (30–60 minutes). People are more likely to attend and pay attention if the sessions aren't overwhelming.

Step 4: Create a PM Community of Practice

One of the most powerful ways to advocate for PM is by fostering a community of practice— a group of like-minded colleagues who regularly meet to discuss and share best practices for managing projects. Here's how you can start:

1. **Set Up Regular Meetings:**
   Whether weekly, biweekly, or monthly, hold regular meetings where team members can discuss ongoing projects, challenges, and lessons learned. This isn't a "lecture"—it's a space for everyone to learn and grow together.

2. **Share Success Stories:**
   Ask participants to share what's working for them. The more people see the benefits of using PM practices, the more they'll be motivated to adopt them.

3. **Promote Open Communication:**
   Encourage everyone to share their experiences and ask questions. You can even create a Slack channel or email list where team members can continue the conversation outside of meetings.

4. **Celebrate Progress:**
      Recognize individuals or teams who have successfully implemented PM techniques. Celebrate their achievements and highlight how PM practices contributed to their success.

Step 5: Influence Organizational Change

Once your colleagues are on board with PM, it's time to think bigger—how can you influence your entire organization? Here's how you can drive positive change on a larger scale:

   1. **Advocate for PM Processes at the Organizational Level:**
      If your company doesn't have formal project management processes, advocate for the introduction of basic PM structures—like defining project phases or setting up a centralized task tracking system. Start small, and show how the changes improve efficiency.
   2. **Speak to Leadership:**
      If you have the opportunity, talk to leaders about the benefits of adopting PM practices. Use data or real-life examples from your team to show how these methods can boost results and reduce risk.
   3. **Create a PM Training Program:**
      Work with HR or training departments to create a PM training program for all employees. The more people who are trained in project management, the more seamless your organization's projects will run.

Final Thoughts: Your Journey as a PM Advocate

Becoming a Project Management advocate doesn't happen overnight. It takes passion, patience, and perseverance. But by starting small, sharing knowledge, and leading by example, you can gradually transform your team, department, and organization into a project management-driven culture.

Remember: you don't need to be the most experienced person in the room to make a difference. By simply sharing what you know and inspiring others, you'll be helping everyone work smarter, not harder. So, go ahead—take the plunge into advocacy. Your team will thank you, and your organization will thrive!

You've already mastered the fundamentals. Now, it's time to help others discover how powerful project management can be. Get ready to make a lasting impact!

CHAPTER 22: CONCLUSION: EMPOWERING NON-PROJECT MANAGERS

Congratulations! You've reached the final chapter, and if you've made it this far, you've already taken a huge step toward mastering the core principles of project management. Whether you're a marketing professional, a team leader, or someone just looking to stay more organized at work and in your personal life, you now have the tools and insights to apply project management strategies that can truly transform the way you work.

But don't just stop here. This is only the beginning. Let's take a moment to recap the key takeaways and offer some final inspiration as you embark on your journey to become a more empowered, efficient, and successful professional.

Key Takeaways: Empowering Non-Project Managers with Project Management Principles

1. **Project Management Is for Everyone**
   Whether or not your title includes "project manager," you already deal with projects every day. By learning how to approach tasks methodically and applying project management principles, you can make your work—and your life—run more smoothly. The techniques covered in this book, from setting clear

objectives to tracking progress, are tools anyone can use.

2. **Effective Communication Is Key**
One of the most powerful lessons from project management is that communication makes or breaks a project. Whether you're sending an email, having a team meeting, or presenting an idea, being clear, concise, and proactive is crucial for making things happen. By mastering communication strategies, you'll build stronger relationships and better team cohesion.

3. **Planning Is a Game-Changer**
Planning isn't just about creating schedules—it's about setting yourself (and your team) up for success. Break projects into manageable tasks, prioritize based on importance, and track progress regularly. This kind of strategic thinking will help you stay on top of your work and avoid unnecessary stress.

4. **The Power of Flexibility and Adaptability**
Not every project goes according to plan, and that's perfectly okay. The key to success is how you adapt when things change. Whether you're using Waterfall or Agile methodologies, understanding when to adjust and how to troubleshoot challenges is what will keep you moving forward, no matter the circumstances.

5. **Teamwork and Accountability Drive Results**
Projects are rarely a solo effort, and when you work with others, it's essential to create a culture of accountability. Assigning clear roles and responsibilities, using collaborative tools, and encouraging open feedback can elevate the performance of any team. The more you understand team dynamics and how to harness collective strengths, the more successful you'll be.

6. **Reflection is the Key to Growth**
After every project (or personal task), take the time to reflect. What went well? What could be improved next

time? This process of continuous improvement helps you refine your approach, boosts your confidence, and prepares you for bigger and better projects in the future.

Final Inspiration: Embrace Project Management to Excel Professionally and Personally

Now that you've mastered the basics, it's time to start applying these principles in your own unique way. Whether you're leading a team, managing personal goals, or navigating complex tasks at work, you have the tools to excel.

But here's the thing: project management isn't just about checking off boxes or managing deadlines. It's about cultivating a mindset of efficiency, focus, and resilience. By embracing these skills, you're not just managing projects—you're setting yourself up for long-term success.

Think about it: project management is about more than just getting things done. It's about creating systems that help you work smarter, not harder. It's about making sure that every task, every project, and every goal aligns with your broader purpose—whether in your career, your personal life, or in the way you interact with others.

So, take a moment to look at your goals—both professional and personal—and think about how project management can help you achieve them. Will you break them down into manageable phases? Will you prioritize what's most important? Will you be proactive in tracking your progress and adjusting along the way?

Now, imagine where these skills could take you. Imagine the confidence you'll have when you can confidently plan, execute, and reflect on your goals. The results won't just be projects completed on time. They'll be achievements that are more aligned with your true potential.

You've already taken the first step by embracing these principles. Now, keep going. Don't wait for the perfect project or opportunity to practice your new skills—start applying them today. You have the power to transform not only your professional life but your personal growth as well.

So, here's to you: the empowered, organized, and strategic non-project manager who's ready to tackle anything that comes your way. Get out there and start applying these principles. The world of project management is at your fingertips, and it's time to unlock your full potential. The best part? You've got this!

In Closing

It's been an exciting journey through the world of project management, and we hope you're feeling equipped and inspired to take on any project that comes your way. Remember, project management isn't about being perfect—it's about progress. Keep learning, keep refining, and, most importantly, keep applying what you've learned.

Here's to your continued success, both at work and in life. The power of project management is now in your hands—go ahead and make things happen!

REFERENCES

Adkins, L. (2010). Coaching Agile Teams: A Companion for ScrumMasters, Agile Coaches, and Project Managers in Transition. Addison-Wesley Professional.

Anderson, D. J. (2010). Kanban: Successful Evolutionary Change for Your Technology Business. Blue Hole Press.

Brown, J., & Hyer, N. L. (2010). Managing Projects: A Team-Based Approach. McGraw-Hill Education.

Cobb, C. G. (2011). Making Sense of Agile Project Management: Balancing Control and Agility. Wiley.

Gantt, H. L. (1910). Work, Wages, and Profits. Engineering Magazine Company.

Kerzner, H. (2017). Project Management: A Systems Approach to Planning, Scheduling, and Controlling (12th ed.). Wiley.

Lencioni, P. (2002). The Five Dysfunctions of a Team: A Leadership Fable. Jossey-Bass.

Project Management Institute. (2021). A Guide to the Project Management Body of Knowledge (PMBOK® Guide) (7th ed.). Project Management Institute.

Reinertsen, D. G. (2009). The Principles of Product Development Flow: Second Generation Lean Product Development. Celeritas

Publishing.

Smith, G. (2018). The Project Manager's Survival Guide: The Top 10 Things You Need to Know to Get by and Thrive. CreateSpace Independent Publishing Platform.

Sutherland, J. (2014). Scrum: The Art of Doing Twice the Work in Half the Time. Crown Business.

Trellis, J., & Vaughn, C. (2020). Managing Multiple Projects: Balancing Priorities and Building Productivity. Productivity Press.

Wysocki, R. K. (2019). Effective Project Management: Traditional, Agile, Extreme (8th ed.). Wiley.

WEB REFERENCES

Agile Alliance. (2001). Manifesto for Agile Software Development. Retrieved from https://agilemanifesto.org.

Trello. (n.d.). Trello Project Management Tool. Retrieved from https://trello.com.

Asana. (n.d.). Asana Project Management Platform. Retrieved from https://asana.com.

ABOUT THE AUTHOR

Gitangshu Adhikary is a seasoned professional with over two decades of experience in streamlining workflows, managing complex projects, and empowering individuals to unlock their potential. With a background in organizational strategy and a passion for simplifying intricate processes, Gitangshu has dedicated his career to bridging the gap between theory and practice in project management.

Throughout his journey, Gitangshu has worked with diverse teams across industries, witnessing firsthand how effective project management principles can transform not just projects but also people. His approach emphasizes practical strategies, accessible tools, and a mindset that even non-project managers can adopt to excel in their roles.

An avid writer and speaker, Gitangshu excels at breaking down complex concepts into relatable, actionable advice. He is committed to helping professionals of all levels master the art of organization, improve collaboration, and achieve their goals with confidence.

When he's not writing or working on projects, Gitangshu enjoys exploring innovative productivity tools, mentoring aspiring leaders, and finding inspiration in everyday challenges.

Project Management Unleashed: A Guide for Non-Project Managers to Organize and Excel is his latest endeavor to empower readers to embrace project management as a transformative life skill.

www.ingramcontent.com/pod-product-compliance
Lightning Source LLC
Chambersburg PA
CBHW071401220526
45469CB00004B/1135